Why I Live

Why I Live

Personal Testimonies of a Doctor
of Metaphysical Science in Cosmic
Consciousness, Chakra Activation
Near Death Experience & More

LIONEL MAITHRI

Library of Congress Control Number: 2004098358
ISBN: Hardcover   978-1-4134-7459-6
                     Softcover   978-1-4134-7458-9

This book was printed in the United States of America.

To order additional copies of this book,
contact:
Xlibris Corporation
1-888-795-4274
www.Xlibris.com
Orders@Xlibris.com
23306

Contents

Preface 7

Introduction 11

PART ONE: SIGNIFICANT LANDMARKS IN MY LIFE

Chapter 1: My Childhood 19
Chapter 2: Higher Education 27
Chapter 3: Public Service in Sri Lanka
            1952 1975 23 years 30
Chapter 4: International Civil Service
            1975 1992 17 years 50
Chapter 5: Retirement in USA 61

PART TWO: Ventures With Teachers And Teachings

Chapter 6: Hinduism A Living Cosmos 81
Chapter 7: Buddhism The Four
            Noble Truths 84
Chapter 8: Christianity Path to Salvation........ 87
Chapter 9: Islam 90
Chapter 10: Gurdjieff & Ouspensky
            Waking up from sleep 93
Chapter 11: Subud Guidance to Find the
            Right Path 98

Chapter 12: Sathya Sai Baba.........................106
Chapter 13: Some Other Spiritual Paths 108

PART THREE: MY SPIRITUAL EXPERIENCES

Chapter 14: My Experience of Cosmic
            Consciousness...........................119
Chapter 15: Chakra Activation.....................130
Chapter 16: Near Death Experience 146
Chapter 17: Experience in Kataragama
            vortexes.....................................153
Chapter 18: Other Remarkable Experiences in
            My Life......................................159

PART FOUR: SYNTHESIS

Chapter 19: My Worldview...........................178
Chapter 20: Why We Live – Lessons of
            Experience................................228

Appendix 1:Detailed Contents – Analytical
            Table..239
Appendix 2:Some Recommended Books...249
From the Author....................................257

Preface

It is with utmost pleasure that I present this book to the world of readers. I have written many technical papers connected with my work for the Government of Sri Lanka and International organizations like the United Nations Development Fund and Commonwealth Fund, but this is the first time I am writing about my own personal experiences. I cannot even remember when I first planned to write. Both my parents being teachers, I grew up in an environment of books. As my father was the headmaster of a school in Sri Lanka, in which my mother was an assistant teacher, we lived in the staff bungalow within the campus, and to me the whole school, which had about thousand students, was like an extension to my house. I loved books more than anything else and distinctly remember imagining that I might one day write some of them. Although I had this dream of writing ever so often I was held back due to a number of reasons. I had always been pressed for time, first with my studies and then with my professional work. After retirement I had no such excuses but then I was already in my seventies, I started wondering whether there is a real need to write as hundreds of writers are producing excellent books on all possible subjects. I read vigorously on my favorite topics such as comparative religion, metaphysics, esoteric knowledge, methods for self-development and spiritual progress. I was both happy and not happy. I must say even with much reluctance that much of what I read appeared to me to be shallow, lacking in the deep and solid authenticity I have seen in my work with the Gurdjieff system, Raja Yoga and most of all in my own childhood epiphany, and later in my Near Death Experience. In spite of my disappointment I felt unequal to the task of writing a book on my experiences, and getting it published. Although I had a large collection of my journals and notes written at different times and had made several attempts to put them together as a book, I felt unequal to the task of writing a book on my own experiences and getting it published. One day I decided to close this exercise. On the following day my attention was drawn to a paragraph in Ken Wilber's ONE TASTE, which showed me without any doubt the difference between transformative and translative material and the obligation of all who have benefited from direct spiritual revelations to communicate their experiences to the world. In Ken Wilber's words: "Because, you see, . . . the alarming fact is that any realization of depth carries a terrible burden: Those who are allowed to see are simultaneously saddled with the obligation to communicate that vision in no uncertain terms: that is the bargain. You were allowed to see the truth under the agreement that you would communicate it to others (that is the ultimate meaning of the bodhisattva vow). And therefore, if you have seen, you simply must speak out. Speak out with compassion, or speak out with angry wisdom, or speak out with skilful means, but speak out you must. Knowing that I have had direct spiritual experiences, and considering my deep respect for Ken Wilber's writings, I could have no further excuses. I decided to start writing immediately. After testing myself with a small website, www. whylive.net, I started writing this book in earnest, with the assistance of my dear wife.

Introduction

While living as human beings we have to be thankful for the earth we are living in and the air we breathe. If we continue to think further we can make a long list of things for which we have to be thankful, because if they were absent our life would have been impossible. As we take for granted many of these things we may not even be aware of them. The earth provides our food and water, gravity makes it possible for us to walk and the seasons provide a picturesque background for our fun activities. Plants provide oxygen that is essential for life and photosynthesis captures sunlight to be stored as starch in our vegetables and cereals. We are thankful to our parents for bringing us to this world, and to relations, neighbors and friends for their affection and companionship. We can go on and on, as we might attempt somewhat in future chapters. We have many debts as well as obligations. We need to recognize the unity of life. We have a sacred obligation to realize that everything we see around us, whether they are plants animals or human beings, moons, planets or suns, are parts of the same cosmic oneness of which human beings are a key element. All these come to our mind when we ask the question why I live, or what am I living for?

The essence of human life is growth and self-development. In the rapidly changing environment of the present times it is quite easy to be carried off the track by unforeseen distractions, which interrupt one's own self-development plans and processes. A determined effort is required to formulate a progressive plan for self-development and adhere to it. This needs a high degree of self-awareness and constant discipline. The resulting reward of a joyful life of peace and contentment is well worth the effort. The author, having lived with contentment for over seven decades, wishes to share his noteworthy experience in this book. Here he reveals for the first time how a vision of the hidden patterns of life forms and processes in the cosmos was revealed to him in an epiphanic experience, and how he utilized that knowledge for his own self-development. His accounts of his experiences in many countries that he visited in the course of his work serve as a case study for those with similar interests. Why I Live is a challenge to all readers to live one's own life in the best possible manner. Life is best managed as an ongoing venture or project. It is one's Atman Project in which each person plays the role of project manager. In a complex project the project manager has to identify the network of interrelated activities, and the significant landmarks. The path of self-development is often represented as one of suffering and self-sacrifice. That has not been my experience. It could lead one to a life of unlimited joy. However it is true that for a serious venture into the higher realms of self-development one often needs some review and reorientation of the normal life we are used to. This observation is based on my own life experience and need not be taken to mean that a sudden change of lifestyle is needed to benefit from this book. Any change in my life style was very gradual, almost imperceptible to others. What I am referring to is a need for determination and an inner orientation as if one is launching a project of inner development. Some of the means at our disposal to gradually reorient our behavior are smiling, sharing whatever good things we possess, simple actions to make someone happy, and engaging in solitary prayer and meditation.

Two of the easily recognized signs of progress, which I experienced in my own life are described below. They were important to me as indications that I was on the correct path. The first is that you gradually stop worrying unnecessarily. Instead of being depressed with endless mental tensions as before, you start feeling relaxed, and at peace accompanied by feelings of joy. You cease to worry about trivial details in your life. When this happens you should feel confident that you are making progress on the path of self-development.

The second is the experience of meaningful coincidences, which are generally called synchronicities. For example, I start thinking of someone I have not met for quite some time, and then meet him suddenly in a most unexpected place quite accidentally. It could very well be an accidental coincidence. Yet if you find such coincidences taking place more and more frequently, more than could be accounted for by laws of chance, you could describe them as synchronicity. What is strange is that when you start taking notice of them, they start happening still more frequently as if a higher intelligence wants you to know that you are being taken care of.

A common synchronicity in my experience is the play with numbers. You suddenly notice that you are reading page 333 in a book, then your eyes go to the clock, which reads 3.33. I might wake up at night to find that the time is 12.34 and this repeats itself the following night. This kind of synchronicity is quite frequent in my life, and

I feel an immense joy recognizing my closeness to a higher intelligence. What is strange is that I can never do it at will. If I look at the clock expecting to find a synchronicity, I never find it. Synchronicity could manifest in so many ways. An unusual thought could come to your head, and the next moment you see an article on the same topic in the newspaper. When the occurrence of such experiences become more and more frequent, you have reason to be happy that your spirituality is developing.

Being fully aware of one's synchronicities is an easy and effective way of strengthening one's links with Higher Intelligence. Simple synchronities are often followed by more complicated ones. In the eighteenth chapter of this book I have related several stories about remarkable synchronicities in my life.

PART ONE

SIGNIFICANT LANDMARKS IN MY LIFE

Chapter I

My Childhood

I was born in Sri Lanka in 1928, while the country was still a colony under British rule. Sri Lanka was called Ceylon at that time as the word Sri Lanka, which is the proper name of the country for about 2500 years, was felt to be difficult for Western tongues, and therefore had to be changed to Ceylon, which they could pronounce more comfortably. The use of nicknames for colonies of European imperial powers was common in Asian and African countries. Serendip was a still earlier abbreviation (by Arab traders) for Sri Lanka Deepa (deepa is the Sinhala word for island). It is from this word Serendip that the English word serendipity was later derived. Serendipity means good luck or good fortune, unearned and unexpected. In the novel Three Princes of Serendip by Horace Walpole the princes had the faculty of finding desirable objects by accident, which may be an allusion to the possibility of discovering, extremely valuable gemstones including sapphires, on or close to the ground surface in some parts of Sri Lanka. Export of gemstones is one of the main sources of revenue of the country even up to the present day.

Sri Lanka, which came under Portuguese rule in the sixteenth century, and Dutch rule in the seventeenth century became a British colony in the eighteenth century. As a child I had an indescribable feeling of oppression when I learned that my country is ruled by foreigners. When independence was regained in 1948 I felt as if a great burden had fallen off my shoulders. Both my parents were teachers. While my father worked as Headmaster of one of a chain of Methodist schools scattered over the country, my mother worked as a teacher, invariably in the same school. Father was entitled to occupy the Headmasters bungalow, which was normally within the school campus. As long back as I could remember our house was always full of books. I sometimes wonder whether my love of books and reading was due to my being surrounded by books from childhood.

As a child I was extremely inquisitive and had a burning desire to understand the meaning of everything I came across. I have a strange feeling and good reason to believe that my faculties of consciousness and memory were active even before my birth. I have a faint memory of listening to voices from inside my mother's womb before I was born, voices becoming louder and then fading off. Even if my faculties of hearing were fully developed sometime before the actual event of birth, how did I know they were human voices? Why was I so elated while listening to them? The possible answer is that these voices brought back memories from my previous births. However, I had to pay a price for my precocious and over-sensitive nature. Traumatic experiences of a prolonged and difficult birth process, as I discovered later, had left their mark on my consciousness leading to frightening dreams of being trapped in a dark tunnel, without knowing how to escape. These dreadful dreams continued through my childhood and even later. It was much later in my forties that I succeeded in clearing these birth traumas, at some transpersonal workshops conducted by a team of psychologists, which I chanced to attend as a part of my training to be a trainer, by sheer synchronicity. I learned that clearing such childhood and pre-birth traumas play an important role in transpersonal development I remember being breastfed by my mother when very young. I can also remember some of the lullabies sung by my father as he carried me. These are some of my most cherished memories. However there were times when I felt that I do not belong here. I was precocious and asked endless questions from my parents and friends and from virtually everybody I met. I pestered everybody with my insatiable thirst for knowledge. Although the more intelligent of them enjoyed talking to me, others became impatient and showed their annoyance openly. I knew all the fifty-two letters, of my mother tongue Sinhala, as well as the twenty-six letters of the English language long before I went to school. Sinhala is an Indo-Aryan language and preserved all the vowels and consonants of Sanskrit although the script is not the same. When later I started exploring other religious systems the meaning and scope of the word God seemed to expand to accommodate all religious systems without any partiality to a particular religion. To me the word God always meant and still means the Supreme Head and Creator of the entire cosmos. At that time I had very few friends. I loved to be alone with my books. I had a deep concern for being right in whatever decision I took. I had three aunts, two unmarried sisters of my mother and an unmarried sister of my father who took turns looking after me. I loved them dearly. Aunty Rosalind who was well educated in English taught me many English words. I enjoyed so much when she took me out in the evening and taught me to sing Twinkle, Twinkle, Little Star, while looking at the stars, which I fancied as strange beings looking at us. In spite of receiving love from everybody, I had a strange feeling that I do not belong here.

At the age of seven I had a spiritual experience of expanded consciousness, of the type normally described as cosmic consciousness. It was a powerful experience which started by my being engulfed by a powerful cloud of life. More important than the the ecstacy to which I was transported instantly, it gave me a new and expanded worldview and a higher source of knowledge which transformed the rest of my life. This experience is fully described and explained in chapter 14. I know for certain that the main events of my life during the next half century, taking me to unexpected heights of professional success and mental and spiritual development would not have been possible without this momentum. Although my inner life was completely changed by this experience, my main frustration at that time was my inability to verbalize what I experienced. When I discovered that I had received a valuable gift of understanding to which others were blind, I had to learn to keep my thoughts secret and adopt a type of playacting to keep all communications smooth and pleasant. I seemed to be living a double life with a yearning for solitude. It took me some time to realize the immensity of what happened to me. The impact of this experience on my later life was quite remarkable. It changed my worldview and made me to believe very firmly that we are all living elements of a cosmos that is alive. In short most of the spiritual experiences that I have described in this book may not have been possible without that experience and its sequels.

I remember I was touching a yellowed cinnamon leaf immediately before the experience. In my mind I had the feeling that I had spent hours there. Although I knew that I had gone through a strange experience my mind was crystal clear. The cosmos was alive with its celestial galaxies, and so were all the elements that merged together to form it, human, animal, vegetable and mineral. Every thing that I perceived, soil, rocks, trees, animals, human beings, planets and the sun were alive and were made of the same tiny particles or building blocks, which were alive too. The first thought that came to me was the similarity of the pattern to an enormous Lego set, with the difference that every small unit and every assembled combination was equally alive. As I had problems with communicating my experience to parents and seniors, I stopped talking to them about it for some time. However I was determined to learn more about those subjects independently. While I somewhat distanced myself from elders temporarily, I spent more time with nature, learning the ways of trees and plants, insects and animals, a whole paradise of variegated life. I enjoyed exploring the secret life of plants and animals and did not mind being described as introvert. Fortunately no one was interested enough to ask me any further questions. The Experience bestowed on me numerous direct and indirect benefits. One of the most significant benefits was in the field of education. My desire to pursue knowledge, my quality of intelligence and my power of retention improved enormously. I scored higher marks in all my subjects. When my father found my renewed interest in education and my high grades in schoolwork, he planned to send me to a higher grade English School A teacher in that school who knew my father agreed to keep me in his home as a paying guest and also to help me in my studies. This gave a further boost to my studies. The teacher was an avid reader and brought books from the school library. Very often to his great surprise I finished reading them before he did. However being away from home was an agonizing experience. David Copperfield, by Charles Dickens became my favorite book because David s experiences were so close to mine. I had a great fear that my mother would pass away when I was not at home and cried at night whenever this dreadful thought came to me. I slept in an outer room and felt very lonely at the beginning. I used to read and do my homework till very late at night. One day I finished my work and came to my bed and on some impulse lifted my sheet high, and was terrified to see a large snake coiled up under the sheet, which happened to be a poisonous cobra. I benefited from the incident by being given an inner room in which I was not so lonely. I completed my Senior School Certificate, the highest class in that school, in my thirteenth year. Thereafter I joined Holy Cross College in Kalutara for my Higher School Certificate and University Entrance classes. I made good use of the more advanced library in this school to search for further knowledge of the revelations in my experience. I gathered a lot of broad knowledge, which helped me in my examinations, although not exactly what I needed for authenticating my revelations.

Chapter 2

Higher Education

Although Holy Cross College admitted me to the University Entrance and Higher School Certificate Examination classes, they experienced problems in recruiting qualified teaching staff. I obtained the syllabuses for the subjects I had selected and started a program of self-study by myself. Whenever I had an opportunity I discussed with students attending schools in neighboring towns. I was encouraged to find that I had covered even more ground than they had. I had absolutely no hopes of passing. However, when the results were released I was so surprised as I was the only arts faculty student who had passed both examinations and I was ready to join the University in my seventeenth year. There was a bill in Parliament to provide free education up to University level; the first country in the world to do so at that time. The law went through and I was extremely happy about it. However it was an uphill task for me, as I had no proper preparation to follow the University study programs. However with considerable effort I managed to pass all the tests. The convocation was a great event for my parents and me and I was extremely happy being able to give them that joy because at that time, being a graduate was a high achievement ensuring high-level employment in the public sector or the private sector.

It is customary for graduates to sit for the Civil Service Competitive Examination if they were still under 25 years of age. Sri Lanka followed the British system of recruiting for the most important positions in the public service through competitive examinations. All precautions were taken to ensure the integrity of this examination, for example by getting the answer papers corrected both in Sri Lanka and in British Universities. I was only twenty-four years oldand thus had two chances to sit for this examination. As only about ten are normally selected to fill the vacant posts in the Civil Service, to which belonged the best public service jobs in the country, I lacked confidence and was not so enthusiastic. I joined as a teacher in a reputed school close by and missed the first chance. Some months later I met one of my University colleagues quite accidentally one morning and he felt shocked to hear that I had not applied to sit for the Civil Service Competitive examination for which the final date for submitting applications was the following day. I rushed home and explained all this to my father and he gave me the money required for the application fee. I sat for the examination and tried to brush it off my mind as I felt it was beyond my ability to perform well enough to be placed within the first ten candidates. A few months later, I was greatly surprised to find that I had been called for the interview, which meant that I had come within the top-most one fourth of the candidates. The vice-chancellor of the University headed the interview board and the interview lasted for nearly one hour. Some time later, to my surprise I was informed that I had been placed seventh in the competitive examination. I was sent a list of ten government jobs to indicate my preferences. I selected the position of Assistant Commissioner of Local Government mainly because I knew that it involved working with the people in rural areas, in contrast to most of the other positions that were bureaucratic office jobs, with no contact with the outside world.

Chapter 3

Public Service in Sri Lanka
1952 1975 23 years

I had to follow a short period of training for the position of Assistant Commissioner of Local government at the Ministry of Local Government Headquarters in the capital of Colombo. As I was the only recruit for this position that year, I was given the freedom to visit the different sections of the Ministry office and acquaint myself with Local government administration in Sri Lanka by discussing with the senior staff. Since no schedules were fixed I was free to do what I liked. This gave me an opportunity to visit during my free time the Ramakrishna Mission in Colombo, which had a very large collection of spiritual books on all the spiritual paths. Ramakrishna was to me the most enlightened spiritual teacher

I knew about because he respected all religions equally. Below his life-like marble statue in the meditation hall were his words "The Truth is One. Sages call it by different names. I may have spent more time reading his talks and writings than Local Government Administration, which was my assigned task. I remember I bought a set of books by Ramakrishna's foremost disciple Vivekananda on different types of Yoga, which are Hatha Yoga (physical development), Jnana Yoga (mental development) Bhakthi Yoga (emotional and devotional activities), Karma Yoga (service to mankind) and Raja Yoga (higher meditation). These books were my constant companions during the many travels to different parts of the country as a part of my inaugural training. As the second phase of training I was assigned to assist in the office of the Assistant Commissioner of Local Government (ACLG) in Ratnapura. The senior ACLG, from whom I was to obtain training, was a very high-ranking officer whose next position was the Chief Officer in Charge of the Capital City of Colombo. He taught me all aspects of the job and gradually entrusted me with increasing responsibilities so that I could take over the administrative functions when he leaves. Ratnapura is the gemming area of Sri Lanka, and I always had an ambition of living there for some time. This was the opportunity I was waiting for. Whenever I could find the time I visited the mines, which were mostly only a few feet deep. There was no comparison to the diamond mines, which I could visit later in Botswana. From time immemorial Sri Lanka has been famous for gem minerals of extremely high quality and uniqueness, so that the island was called Ratnadvipa meaning The Island of Gems. I managed to follow a short course on gemology to be able to understand the basics of the industry. The gem fields are largely confined to alluvial soils deposited by large rivers in this part of the country. However valuable gems have been found almost in all parts of the country, justifying the use of the word serendipity. The most celebrated Sri Lanka gems, which are in high demand for export, are Blue sapphires, Cat s Eyes, Rubies, Alexandrites, Moonstones, Zircons, Garnets, Amethysts and Topaz. Ability of the gem mining industry to continue for well over 2500 years without causing major environmental problems rests on the unique traditional mining methods. The gems are mined by panning gravel obtained either by making shallow pits not exceeding 10 to 12 feet or by extraction of riverbed gravel. The age-old traditional technology is simple and small scale and works on a unique system of cooperative profit sharing. The export income from gems mined using traditional mining methods, is over 60% of the total income from all mining products.

My next transfer was to Matale, a town to the North of the Hill capital Kandy. It was at the Aluvihara rock Temple just north of Matale that in the 2nd century BC, the Buddhist scriptures known as the Tripitaka were first committed to writing. This was a gigantic task that required the endeavor of hundreds of monks. The massive volume of the Buddhist scriptures was up to that time preserved by committing them to memory. This practice was called the bhanaka system. Different groups of monks in different temples preserved different sections of the Buddhist scripture in three volumes called the "Three Baskets" or Tripitaka by memory. On full moon days the text is chanted melodiously in a ceremony called Pirith, which is held in a beautifully constructed structure. A white thread connects the chanting priests seated within the structure (Pirith Mandapaya) to all those who are listening. After the chanting, which could take the whole night; pieces of the spiritually charged thread are tied round the wrists of listeners for blessings and protection from disease and evil influences. I was able to visit this temple many times to have discussions with the monks. I enjoyed my work as for the first time I was solely in charge of the Assistant

Commissioner's Office and the administration of Local government Authorities in the region. There are four types of Local Authorities in Sri Lanka, which are Municipal Councils for the largest Cities, Urban Councils for large towns, Town Councils for smaller towns and Village Councils for rural areas. The duties of an Assistant Commissioner of Local government (ACLG) are related to the control of Local Governments by the Central Government. I was an officer of the Central Government and ensuring that funds disbursed to local governments by the central government are used properly is one of the major responsibilities of the ACLG. Inquiries into allegations are sometimes very complicated as lawyers normally defended chairmen, whereas ACLGs who had to handle the prosecution could not obtain the assistance of lawyers. Another difficult function was presiding at the elections of new chairmen or mayors at politically charged meetings, which could be very crowded and tense. The job of an ACLG involved much traveling, sometimes on foot, to very remote areas. Once I had to go on foot to a hilly region called Laggala, and was impressed by the beautiful landscape. After a number of inspections of newly constructed public utilities such as wells and culverts on foot, we left the village to go back to our jeep. There were three of us, myself, an officer from my office and the driver. After a long walk we realized that we had lost our way. We walked on till we could find somebody to get directions. The first person we met warned us that we have strayed into bear territory, infested with wild animals, and gave us directions to find our way. We had to walk a very long distance. At one place we had to cross a stream with clear water. As my feet were aching I removed my shoes and socks and dipped my feet in the water. I felt refreshed and after some time we could find our jeep and we got home. At night I felt a burning sensation on my feet and legs and looked at my feet. My legs and feet were covered by large black spots almost like tattoo marks. Those spots were velvety to the touch. As it was quite late by that time I had to wait till morning to go to the doctor. He examined me and confirmed that a tiny insect or mite, which are normally found on the bodies of wild animals. had attacked me. He said they could penetrate the organs of the body through blood vessels, in which case it could be fatal. He kept me in the hospital for a day and gave me several injections and smeared the affected parts with an ointment. Fortunately they cleared in two days. He told me that they could have caused my death. Those who heard the story said that the stream where I removed my shoes could be the haunt of wild animals such as bears and said that

I was lucky to save my life from such wild animals even more than from the tiny mites.

Galle, a town situated about 70 miles south of the capital Colombo was my next station. The major attraction of the town were the beautiful beaches and the Dutch fort which were surrounded by a great variety of landscapes varying from beaches to marsh lands to dry planes to hills. To add to the natural beauty, Galle has a great history too. History of this township and port goes back to King Solomon's time. It is believed that Galle was the ancient seaport "Tarshish", from which king Solomon imported ivory, gems and other valuables. It had been the most prominent seaport in the country, in the period before the commencement of western rule. Persians, Arabs, Greeks, Romans, Malays and Indians were doing business through Galle port. The 'modern' history of Galle starts in 1505, when the first Portuguese ship anchored in the Galle harbor. In 1597, the south-western region of Sri Lanka, including Galle, was captured by the Portuguese. The Portuguese had to surrender to the Dutch armies who took over Galle in 1638. It was they who built the Fort in 1663, in the way it is seen now. They built a fortified wall, using solid granite, and built three bastions, called the sun, moon and star. There was a developed town center, and a whole lot of buildings. When the British took over the country from the Dutch, in 1796, they kept the Fort unchanged, and had it as the administration center of Galle. In addition to the nice beaches, Galle is also famous for handicrafts and, mostly, jewelry. As this was a large district my work was quite heavy. I could still devote considerable time for social and charitable work and became an active member of the YMCA. My official duties as Assistant Commissioner of Local Government included the involvement of local governments and rural communities in rural development work. My visits to the poor communities showed me how much of development work was needed in the villages.

The Junior Chamber International (JCI) had been introduced to Sri Lanka at this time and the first chapter in the capital city of Colombo was receiving much attention on account of the community development work accomplished by them in the low-income communities within and adjacent to the city. JCI was a fast growing international network at that time with chapters in many developed countries such as the United States and United Kingdom and spreading into developing countries such as India, Malaysia and Sri Lanka. JCI members are 18- to 40-year-old professionals and entrepreneurs who join a local JCI chapter. Creating positive change is the main focus of their activities. Leadership training at all levels is an area of high priority. I was impressed by the work being done by Jaycees in Colombo and joined a group of public servants and professionals including young lawyers and businessmen who were willing to form a local chapter of Jaycees in this city. At the inaugural meeting I was elected to the Executive Committee of the new Jaycee chapter as the Treasurer. Our chapter represented several occupations and skills and grew in strength, laying new foundations, and establishing new friendships and networks. I was able to organize seminars and workshops under the auspices of the Junior Chamber, to share and impart my knowledge of management techniques such as Program Evaluation and Review Technique (PERT) and Critical path method (CPM). We started several projects, which included leadership development, skills training, and community development. My main area of interest and involvement was in training camps for low-income children focused on health development. JAYCEE monitors visited low-income households and identified sickly children who were under nourished and had not benefited from government sponsored childcare services due to the neglect of the parents. They were invited to weeklong children s camps during which period they were examined by pediatricians and treated for any diagnosed ailments while being properly groomed with new clothing, skincare, haircuts, nutritional food etc. by trained child care professionals and nurses at the cost of JAYCEES. There were supplementary educational programs in music, dancing and drama. At the end of the period parents were invited to receive advice on proper follow up of program activities under the guidance and support of JAYCEE monitors who continued visits for a period of three months. I could link the follow-up with local community centers for which I was officially responsible. I obtained great happiness in this type of work in which the social benefits were immediately apparent.

After a few years in the Galle district I was transferred to the adjacent district of Matara. My period of work in Matara was one of the most eventful periods in my whole life, for several reasons. I was responsible for starting a JAYCEE chapter in Matara under my leadership, to continue the type of service I performed in the previous district. I was also active with YMCA and the Anti-tuberculosis campaign.

This was the time that the spiritual organization called Susila Budhi Dharma (popularly known as Subud) was introduced to Sri Lanka. It started in Indonesia with a spiritual contact received by Pak Subuh, the founder. My experiences with Subud are related in greater detail in the eleventh chapter. Spiritually guided coincidences played a major role in the way I was brought to this spiritual movement, very similar to my joining the Gurdjieff movement. It is a strange fact that most of those who joined Subud had previously been in Gurdjieff work.

One of the initial problems was that Subud spiritual meetings called by the Indonesian word latihan, meaning exercise, were only held in Colombo, hundred miles North of Matara. I started traveling to Colombo weekly for latihans. Luckily there were two latihans on Sundays, and I was given permission to attend both latihans because I was traveling a long distance. This was a most eventful time for me. After a few months of latihans I was surprised to find in myself several clear signs of physical well-being and even rejuvenation. One of the ailments that bothered me most was a frequent headache. During latihans I felt my scalp moving as if being massaged causing the scalp to glide up and down over the head. It was not an unpleasant feeling although some times there was some concern owing to the strangeness of the experience. I later found that I could move the scalp from side to side voluntarily causing my ears to move forward and backward. Among the benefits obtained by this involuntary scalp massage movement were the healing of my frequent headaches, appearance of hair on two bald patches at my temples, and also the appearance of black hair on some spots where white hair was appearing. These made me feel exceedingly happy not only because they improved my health and appearance, but also because these were benefits that could directly be ascribed to the practice of latihan without any doubt whatsoever. I became determined to do whatever I could to help this new spiritual force to spread as widely as possible. Another far reaching benefit was the ability to use Subud testing to solve personal problems. At the beginning I started using Subud testing even to make trivial decisions and then felt guilty about this till I discovered that I could have a preliminary test to find out whether it would be alright to test. Eventually this made my testing less frequent and more balanced. This undoubtedly was the most powerful manifestation of spiritual energy I had ever encountered in my life. Please see Chapter 11 for more details. Subud membership in Matara increased very rapidly and within two months we had over twenty-five Subud members. The only way they could do latihan weekly was to travel to Colombo by car or by train. I became the unofficial organizer for Subud members in Matara. I gave rides whenever I drove to Colombo for latihan, and arranged rides whenever other members drove to Colombo. Some times whenever the number of those wanting to go was too big, I arranged rides to the railway station on Sunday mornings and return trips from the station in the evenings. On such occasions I had to sacrifice my visits to see my parents during the weekends. When I explained to my parents why I had to interrupt my weekend visits they asked me for details, and later volunteered to join Subud causing me surprise and immense happiness.

Subud helpers in Colombo had consulted Bapak about the growing number of members in Matara. New members were not allowed to practice latihan (this word meant exercises in Indonesian) without the presence of one or more senior members who are called helpers. Bapak had advised helpers in Colombo to go to Matara weekly to enable group latihans to be held in Matara. Eventually two Subud members who had large houses allowed the use of their houses to enable latihans to be held in Matara weekly. We were greatly excited when we heard that Bapak's world tour included a trip to Matara. This meant that so many arrangements had to be done. First of all we had to find a large enough place where all visitors from Colombo too could join in the latihans. I heard that in the heart of the city there was an unoccupied house and visited the building. It was a very large beautifully ornamented upstair house with a garden, where even hundreds could have latihans or meetings. I was unable to find out why it was not occupied, but there were some rumours that the building was haunted. I was extremely happy when I found that a friend of mine in Matara was related to the owner who lived about fifty miles away. I visited my friend and asked whether he could take me to the owner. When I explained to him about Subud, he was very interested and wished to know further details. He took me to see the owner who lived in a beautiful hill station called Deniyaya, surrounded by tea plantations. After obtaining some information about Subud, the owner said it was alright for us to use the building for some time as he had no immediate plans. He agreed to inform the caretakers. I was extremely happy. We started meeting there twice a week for latihans, with helpers from Colombo. We had over forty members on some days. We had latihan from about eight o clock at night, followed by dinner to which members contributed. After that we sat round the visiting helpers and had most interesting discussions in which the helpers related their experiences about the beginnings of Subud and how it is spreading all over the world. Some times the discussions went on till after midnight. In the meantime arrangements for the visit of Bapak and his retinue went on quite smoothly.

Another exciting development at that time was my engagement to Sreeni, my wife. This was made possible by the conversion to Subud of her father, an attorney-at-law with an extremely rationalist mindset, through a chain of incredible events. When my father-in-law heard that his intended son-in-law, which is myself, had joined an obscure religious group called Subud, he wanted to go to the center and find out for himself. I was quite surprised to see him at the subud house one day before a latihan session, and knowing that he had a reputation for aggressive arguments in the law-courts, I was quite concerned. I avoided confronting him and observed from a distance. When he started asking questions, the leader told him that latihan was about to start and he could walk in if he so desires, and ask his questions later. As he walked in, lights were dimmed for the half hour latihan. As he was leaving at the end of the session there were tears in his eyes and he appeared to be in pain. I saw the chairman of the Subud group walking up to him and withdrew. The chairman Tarzie Vittachi, a reputed journalist who later held a senior post in UNICEF, had been close to my father-in-law during latihan, when Vittachi felt a very sharp pain in his left arm. When Tarzie mentioned this to him after the latihan, my father-in-law had told him that he has had a major fracture right at that spot in his arm. Although it had healed properly this day he felt a recurrence of the pain. This was not a great surprise to Vittachi as he had undergone'similar experiences of sharing pain with others. But it made a great impact on my father-in-law who personally recommended that all his three children, including Sreeni should join Subud. This was followed by his own brothers and sister. This made me extremely happy and we had a great wedding. Soon afterwards, both my parents and my brother too, became followers of Subud. Bapak's visit to Matara was a great success. An insignificant incident during his visit greatly strengthened my faith in Subud. We had arranged for Bapak to have lunch at a beautiful house by the seaside, owned by a Subud member. Dinner was arranged at another Subud member's house. When we went to the place where lunch was arranged, Bapak inquired whether we could go to the other house where we intended having dinner to have our lunch, and return to the seaside house for dinner. We all agreed to do so even if it caused some inconvenience as the lunch was already being prepared at this place. When we went to the other house, an Indonesian visitor from Colombo who was the Indonesian Ambassador for Sri Lanka, a very senior Subud member, turned up while we were having lunch. I inquired from him later whether he went to the seaside house before coming here. He denied doing so to my great surprise, as I had left instructions for him at the sea-side house. He had depended on his ability to test, to find the right house. At that time this surprised me very much because I did not know that Subud testing could be used in such situations. A number of seemingly miraculous personal experiences took place in our lives at this time. Soon after our wedding, I had a transfer to another region called Badulla district. We had never travelled to this area, but a colleague of Sreeni who was living at Badulla had agreed to keep us in her home till we found a house. At this time, I was experimenting with the newly discovered Subud testing process whenever I could find an opportunity. Although I was still not certain whether it was correct to test a spiritual process in this way after a test I decided to travel to Badulla and to find Sreeni's friend's house purely by testing, and it worked perfectly. The success we accomplished in this venture increased my faith in Subud and Subud testing a thousand fold. As I acquired greater confidence in this immense spiritual power, I was guided that I should not continue to use it frivolously as during the phase of experimentation. Although I have continued to use this source of energy and guidance up to now, I do it only where the issue in question is extremely important and is beyond solution with my own thinking.

In 1966 I was awarded a Scholarship to England for postgraduate studies in Local Government and Public Administration. My wife too could join me. Apart from the studies we had excellent sight seeing tours in England and France, including visits to subud centers.

My most memorable visit in England was to Coombe Springs, a massive mansion south of London, where J.G. Bennett had the Headquarters of both the Gurdjieff movement and the Subud organization of England. Bennett was an eminent authority and author in physics and mathematics and was the Chairman of the British Coal Board at one time. He used Coombe Springs for Gurdjieff work, subud latihans and also for conducting seminars on high level metaphysical topics, one of which I could attend. He paid special attention to me as a pupil of Professor Ratnasuriya, and recollected how Ratnasuriya took him through the jungles of Nepal to meet Shivapuri Baba, a Hindu saint whom Bennett befriended. Bennett wrote a book called Long Pilgrimage about his visits to Shivapuri Baba, who lived up to 137 years.

On my return from UK to Sri Lanka I fulfilled a long felt ambition to find a job in the field of training at the Academy of Administrative Studies (SLIDA). In the course of training senior civil servants in advanced techniques of administration and management, I organized interactive workshops with institutions like Sarvodaya set up by its founder, Dr. T. Ariyaratne with the objective of improving the level of popular participation in administrative machinery at the rural level in Sri Lanka. He described the main objective of Sarvodaya Organization as a way of awakening the rural masses. A major barrier to village development was the apathy and hopelessness of the poor villagers. The root problem of poverty is a sense of personal and collective powerlessness, and awakening the rural masses had to take place not in isolation but through social, economic, and political interaction.

My experiences during the next few years were quite varied. I had a number of visits to Sri Lankan villages observing how varied patterns of rural development institutions were being provided a solid ideological foundation through the Sarvodaya movement. Thereafter I had a number of visits to foreign countries for receiving training in Higher techniques of management to be used in the training of Sri Lankan civil servants. One of the most challenging was a training program in computerized Network Analysis and Project Evaluation and Review Technique (PERT) at the Cranfield College of Technology in England. This was followed by a Seminar at the International Union of Local Authorities in the Hague, Netherlands, attended by high level local government executives from many parts of the world. The last part of this international study program was in Japan and the Philippines. The first part was at the United Nations Center for Regional Development at Nagoya Japan, where an international team of consultants sat down to draw up a regional development plan for the Bicol Region of the Philippines. During the second part, the planning team including myself, went to the Bicol Region to present the plans formulated by us to the regional development executives in the Philippines. It was a most interesting type of activity spotlighting the varying and conflicting impressions of personnel from different levels of authority, e.g. international, federal, state and local governments on grass-root level realities. This exercise highlighted the need for effective participation at the grassroots levels. On returning from the training program I worked with enthusiasm to impart the advanced knowledge gathered by me to my trainees at the Academy of Administrative Studies. Work at the Academy paved the way for me to fulfill my highest ambition in life by joining the United Nations as a consultant in Local and Regional Development at CAFRAD, the African Center for Regional Development.

Chapter 4

International Civil Service
1975 1992 17 years

In 1975 my first assignment with the United Nations Development Program was at the Center for African Training and Research (CAFRAD), located in Tangier, Morocco. This was funded jointly by the United Nations and the Organization for African Unity (OAU). I planned and supervised a Coordinated Research Program on Local and Regional Government. From its Training Center at Tangier, Morocco, I also had to organize and conduct training programs for local authority elected executives and employees in all African countries. The mission was to eliminate the problems caused by the historical imperialistic heritage of different African countries being administered in three languages, English, French and Arabic, which led to problems in sharing administrative experiences of a region in which three totally different languages and administrative systems prevailed. The strategy was to bring senior administrators to advanced trilingual seminars and workshops held at central spots, usually at large luxury hotels such as Hiltons, using simultaneous interpretation.

Although the work was very hectic, and I was out of home most of the time, I enjoyed being stationed in Morocco. Morocco was a most beautiful country, with an internationally reputed beach, which was incredibly crowded during Summer months. While in Morocco we had the opportunity of visiting Granada in Spain, to see the most beautiful ruins of the Muslim city of Granada (Gharna-tah in Arabic), constructed during the period of the Nasrid Empire, when Muslims ruled the major part of the Iberian Peninsula for eight centuries. It was only in 1492 that the Catholic kings of Castile recaptured the area closing one of the most turbulent and glorious chapters in Islamic history. The Nasrid empire, extending from Spain in the West to North India in the East, contributed to unique experiments in the blending of varied cultural elements in the vast area covered by the empire. For example this blend of European, Arabic and Indian cultures throughout seven centuries of the Nasrid Empire led to the growth of a new form of music called Andalusian music. When we observed that some Andalusian melodies were remarkably similar to Sri Lankan Nurthi music, I did some exploratory research, which revealed that those melodies had been borrowed by Sri Lankans from Indian drama companies touring Sri Lanka. The composers of the drama music had borrowed those melodies from Andalusian music, which spread far and wide from Spain in the West to North India in the East.

The presence of a few but devoted Subud practitioners made a great difference to our life in Morocco. One of them had a very large house in which we could conduct all our subud sessions very comfortably. Latihans which we had in this house and later in a school hall were memorable events and gave us the feeling that the world is a small community; as wherever we were, the spiritually significant events fitted into the picture without any conflict with other activities, and without any need for change.

This brings to mind several earlier experiences of latihans in different countries, for example, the latihans I used to have in Japan with my Japanese subud friends, in quaint Buddhist temples, followed by long sessions of tea drinking, with hardly any conversation but lots of bows and smiles. Once while on a one-day visit to a Swedish city, I picked up a telephone directory in the bedroom at night, and called the phone number for subud. I introduced myself to the lady who answered the phone and when I mentioned the name of my hotel she was very excited and mentioned that her husband was right then at the building adjoining that hotel, where a subud group meeting was planned to be held in ten minutes. She gave me directions for the three-minute walk and promised to call her husband to wait for me. Although it was a very cold night I managed to get there in a few minutes. This synchronicity was such a surprise for all of us, and we spent a long time having coffee and sandwiches to welcome me. I have had similar meetings in other countries such as Netherlands and Norway. As Subud was still new at this time, members cherished such chance meetings with members from other countries and exchange information. Another useful contact I made in Morocco was with a friend who had contacts with a Sufi group. Sufism was an esoteric branch of Islam and I was very interested to obtain direct information with a group. At this time Sufi activities were banned by the Islamic government, as orthodox Muslims considered Sufis to be heretics. Due to this situation I was never able to obtain access to a Sufi meeting, but my friend made many rare Sufi books available to me. In our long discussions we talked about the likelihood of a remote link of subud with Sufism, as Bapak the founder of Subud frequently used Sufi terminology in his talks. This friend also gave me some fascinating information about his friend Robert Temple who wrote "Sirius Mystery: New Scientific Evidence for Alien contact 5,000 Years Ago", a book that expounds a theory that intelligent beings from the star Sirius came to earth and established links with a number of African communities. These communities were still maintaining psychic and telepathic links with each other, and held their newly born children to the star Sirius in the form of an initiation ceremony.

While in Morocco our three children attended the American School of Tangier, based on the American system and almost fully staffed by American teachers. Our decision to send them to an American School at this stage made it easy for them to continue their further studies in American Universities.

In 1982 the Commonwealth Fund for Technical Co-operation appointed me as Staff Development and Training Officer for the Ministry of Local Government in Botswana. I was responsible for human resources development of 6000 employees of local authorities in Botswana. I had to introduce a number of innovative training programs considering the low level of formal education of most of the employees. Although many of them had the required level of skills they lacked formal certification from educational institutions. Sometime before I took over responsibilities, the government had appointed a Commission of Inquiry to investigate into possible remedial measures for this problem. Unfortunately, the members of this Commission were drawn from developed countries that lacked experience in situations in developing countries. After investigation, they had recommended that about one third of the employees who lacked paper qualification should be discontinued and that formal training institutions should be established to train all employees to required levels. I was unable to agree with these recommendations because for discontinuing such a large number of employees without determining their on-the-job levels of skill was a sheer wastage of skilled manpower. In many developing countries, the requirement for holding middle level jobs was levels of skill in performing jobs rather than paper qualifications. There is always a possibility of testing the knowledge levels of existing staff and taking action to upgrade their knowledge levels through inexpensive on-the-job training programs. My solution to the problem was based on such thinking. I planned for the testing of basic knowledge as well as job performance skills. On this basis I could conclude that there was no need to dismiss any of the existing employees. With World Bank and other external funding, a massive on-the-job training program was launched. This consisted of the training of training officers for each local authority in special training programs in which they were given a thorough nine-month training at the Ministry under my supervision using proficient trainers from UK, USA, Sweden etc. I also launched a Mobile Training program using large recreation vehicle type moving classrooms fitted with modern audio-visual training equipment. Special attention was paid to employees in remote areas as the levels of administrative skills in remote areas were found to be intolerably low. It was agreed that through the suggested measures, the level of performance could be upgraded to satisfactory levels within five years. A comprehensive project for the next five years was planned to upgrade performance levels to still higher levels. This was needed as the economy of Botswana was progressing so rapidly, at a pace which was not comparable to any other African country, because Botswana had started developing three of the world's richest diamond minds which gave an unprecedented boost to social and economic development with a comparable increase in the needs of human resource development and training needs of government and local authority employees.

Parallel to the heavy challenges of work in the field of training and staff development, I kept up a suitable pace of effort in my own spiritual development practices such as meditation, enabling good progress in advanced meditation practices.

I also continued to increase my knowledge of astrology by following a correspondence course from the Faculty of Astrological studies in London, England. They even conducted their examinations through the University of Botswana for my benefit and I managed to get through the necessary examination to obtain a certificate in astrology.

No account of Botswana would be complete without reference to the bushmen. The Bushmen of Southern Africa are considered to be the most unique and most ancient of all tribal people in the world. During my life in Botswana in the nineteen eighties and nineteen nineties I had a grand opportunity to observe these people at close range and get acquainted with their culture. Around 3000 years ago they occupied the major part of southern Africa from the river Zambesi in the North to the Cape of Good Hope and from the Atlantic to the Indian Ocean. They are the most intensively studied aboriginal people on earth. Around 75000 bushmen were still surviving in the most inhospitable areas of southern Africa.

The Europeans who invaded Southern Africa 350 years ago found it impossible to communicate with them or to use them for any kind of useful service and treated them as just vermin who could be a threat to their livestock, and started killing them in large numbers. There are unmentionable tales about the means used to get rid of them, such as engaging exterminators to kill them and bring body parts which were exchanged for money. When I was in Botswana in the 80s they were found mostly in the Okavango delta, far removed from all civilization, and still continuing to live their ancient ways of community living. Men went into the surrounding jungle to hunt with bow and arrow and brought back their kill causing jubilation in the whole community, as they skinned and burnt the flesh and devoured the meat in a prolonged feast of singing, eating and dancing. It is said that Bushmen (this word includes the women) could eat sufficiently for a whole week and go on without any food till they get another kill. Their bodies are formed by nature to be able to distend the stomachs for storing fat, somewhat similar to those of camels. In these sessions of feasting they performed their tribal dances, mostly imitating the movements of animals for hours and hours and sometimes throughout the whole night. It is said that in the course of such prolonged singing and dancing sessions, one of the men got into a trance and demonstrated extra sensory perceptions, to recover lost properties or animals, to prescribe herbal remedies for serious ailments, and they even healed the sick by laying hands on the affected parts of the body. After some time, the power was transferred to another person and then to another and so on. However, the Bushmen culture is fast disappearing and by the time my family and I left Botswana in the 1990 s, the way of life had undergone profound changes. Whereas in the 80s, the traditional women dancers did not cover their upper bodies during dance sessions, in the 1990 s, they had become conscious of their nudity and had started wearing leather or cloth garments to cover their upper bodies. Their services were gradually being utilized for employment in cattle farms or other occupations where their ability to survive in the jungle using instincts and traditional means of survival proved to be assets. Large numbers of Bushmen had even been recruited by the regular army and mining Industries. One of the Bushmen s advantages over other people had been their ability to survive without surface water. They had developed traditional means of finding liquid-bearing melons and tubers and their unique practice of burying water-filled ostrich egg-shells during the wet season to be later recovered during drought. Some of their traditional life styles had been utilized as entertainment in the movie "The Gods Must Be Crazy" and its sequels. They also had developed a system of using poisoned arrows in hunting and fighting.

Chapter 5

Retirement in USA

In 1992, I terminated my assignment in Botswana to migrate to USA with the family. We had a very warm welcome from our children who were already living in USA. Without any doubt this was the best period of our lives for the whole family. The climate in California suited us as it was very similar to our country of birth. At last I was completely free of all the stresses of professional work. I had no intentions of looking for work, part-time or full-time. I found this a paradise for book lovers and lost no time familiarizing myself with all the libraries and bookshops close by. In no other country have I seen so many bookshops and libraries open till so late into the night. As I loved sketching and drawing I visited art shops and stocked myself with all varieties of paper and canvasses, and drawing pencils and oil paints.

I decided to further my studies in the fields of comparative religion and metaphysics that were my favorite areas of interest and joined the University of Metaphysics headed by Dr Leon Masters to continue studying for a masters Degree in Metaphysical Sciences. I joined the Kundalini Research Network(KRN) as it was one of my areas of interest. I attended an International Convention of KRN held in Toronto and presented a paper on my meditation and chakra activation experiences, which was highly appreciated at the long discussion that followed. I was happy to complete my Doctoral Degree Program at the University of Metaphysics. I presented a paper on "Kundalini Energy" and another paper on "Why Live" at two of the University of Metaphysics annual conventions. During this period, I was diagnosed to be in need of heart surgery and ended up with a quadruple bypass operation. Something went wrong at this surgery, which threatened my life. I had a near-death experience that proved to be one of the most remarkable spiritual experiences in my life. At this time, a few months after my surgery, Southern California underwent a very severe earthquake, of which we happened to be very close to the epicenter and as a consequence suffered very heavy damage to our belongings. It was perhaps the most traumatic experience in our lives. However we were fortunate to come out of it without serious injury, although I was bruised by a bookshelf which fell on my bed. After the earthquake we moved into Fickett Towers in Van Nuys, an apartment complex in a twelve-story building originally built by the Baptist Church for its senior members. It was a well organized and efficiently managed establishment with a large dining room and an exotic rose garden. The tenants represented diverse cultures making it very homely for us, as we had lived in a large number of different countries before coming to USA, because of my United Nations career. Our familiarity with many languages helped us make friends with many tenants within a short time and our life became very interesting. I had a burning desire to share the knowledge and understanding I had received through my spiritual experiences and revelation, which I could not share with others earlier due to my being engaged in busy programs of academic and professional work. My eagerness to share my experiences kindled the desire to write this book. As a preliminary exercise towards fulfilling this ambition, I setup a website under the name "Why Live"

I played a leading role, to start a weekly Brainstorm Session at Fickett Towers, with a few other interested tenants such as Lillian Smith and Barbara Webb, who was at that time the President of the Tenants Association. Barbara Webb, a retired professor of art, with her deep understanding and experience in varied fields including anthropological and metaphysical sciences gave life to the sessions and also supported me in writing my book in many ways. Our motto was "Use the brain or lose it." In addition to open discussions on a wide range of challenging subjects, we invited speakers from organizations such as universities and Jet Propulsion Laboratory, which is affiliated to NASA. When I became too involved with the writing of this book, Barbara Tiffany took over the responsibility of running the brainstorm sessions. Another organization in which my wife Sreeni and I played an active role was the Sri Lanka Arts and Drama Circle of California headed by the famous drama producer Kalasuri Mudalinayaka Somaratne. While I served as the Secretary of the group for several years, Sreeni supported the group with her musical talents. She had been a radio singer quite early in her life by her association with her father Wilmot Wijetunge, a reputed research scholar in the history of Sri Lankan drama. She illustrated his radio talks by singing classical Nurthi music, until she became a popular radio singer on her own merit. She played the Sitar for some of the plays produced by the Arts and Drama Circle. She is also the co-author of this book.

In August 2004 we left Los Angeles to live in a beautiful and comfortable house owned by our youngest son Senal and daughter-in-law Shelly, overlooking the beautiful Puget Sound area and Everett City, with the perpetually snow covered Mt Baker prominently displayed in the background right in front of the house. It is the house of our dreams. The years we spent in California and Washington in close contact with our children, has been the most enjoyable period in our lives. The credit goes to our three children and their families. Anjali and Guyen our daughter and son-in-law and the two grand daughters intellectually talented Anisha and artistically gifted Leoni have never failed to shower their love on us, surprising us in most unexpected ways. Our two sons and their families, Harindra, Ivana and sweet little Janna show us all their love, while Senal, Shelly and darling Seth the most lovable child on earth, have made our life complete.

Poetry writing was another of my long-desired hobbies. I edited a book of poems by Pantaleon, one of my closest friends, while still a university student. Writing haiku style poems was also one of my favorite hobbies. In USA, I got two of my poems published in the annual poetry collections of the International Library of Poetry for 2001 and 2002.

PART TWO

VENTURES WITH TEACHERS AND TEACHINGS

IIA

Different Paths to self-development

Comparative religion has been one of my favorite areas of study, even from my childhood. I never had any doubt that the founders of all major religions have been sent to this earth by the same Cosmic intelligence, which is God. When, with the passage of time, God saw the need for special assistance in human affairs, in some part of the world, He arranged for a special messenger to come to our world bringing an appropriate set of teachings, like Krishna, Buddha, Abraham, Jesus Christ, Mohammed etc. Their teachings, which were called religions, were most suitable for the time and place and were meant to be understood and acted upon by everybody, but unfortunately people at different levels of understanding and sincerity interpreted them differently. For example, there is not even a single major religion today, which has not got divided into several versions or denominations. This causes problems to sincere students of religion.

In my humble opinion, each living being is a part of the cosmos and may be described as a cell in the cosmos or body of God. All human beings are equal and each of them has to play a specific role in the universe just as each cell in a body has a unique role to play in keeping the body healthy and strong. All parts of the whole, called holons in metaphysical terminology are in communication with God, which is the whole; as well as with all other holons. They are in perfect harmony like an immense orchestra conducted by God, who is aware of every discord. Religious scriptures are full of fascinating stories about God, as the supreme intelligence of the cosmos, helping individuals or groups of individuals in miraculous ways. Monks and nuns who developed personal links with the spiritual domain have written most interesting books about the nature of their intimate experiences on the spiritual path to which they belonged.

When a CEO of a multinational company sends his problem solving experts to different problem spots, would the suggestions one expert formulates for one branch in one country be relevant to another branch in another country? May be not. However they would provide training material as genuine case studies for employees in all branches. It is the same with different religions. They all have a common basis of truth, and could provide useful self development and spiritual development training material for all others if used with understanding. The comments I provide in the following chapters are based on my own direct or indirect experiences of those religions and spiritual paths and are only intended to be autobiographical.

The Zen story of "The finger pointing to the moon" illustrates a common negativity found in religious knowledge and practice. Of many versions of the story, I have selected one, which appeals to me best.

A primary school teacher, in an art class for children, saw the full moon shining through one of the windows. Desirous of involving the children in drawing from life, she called the children to the window, and pointing to the moon with her finger, said Look children what you see there is the moon. Look at it carefully and draw it in your book. She gave them a few minutes and walked round the class looking at their attempts. None of them had drawn a circle as she expected. Full of curiosity to find out what is happening, she questioned the children as to what they were drawing. To her surprise, she found that the children were drawing her finger instead of the moon.

In this story, the moon was God and the finger was the spiritual teacher. When the spiritual teacher attempted to teach about God, the audience paying attention to the teacher s reference to God, mistakenly believed that the teacher was God and started worshipping the teacher more fervently than God. I need not elaborate how true this is in many religions.

Some times these fingers pointing to the one moon are mistaken to be different moons, causing misunderstandings that distort the harmonious nature of the teachings. Some followers resorted to breaking away and forming reformed branches, while the more spiritual preferred to get away from organized religion and formed esoteric groups. However all teachings which originated from the Creator were of utmost value.

Antagonism towards other religions was greatest in those who were at lower levels of spiritual development. As they developed spiritually, they began to realize the truths contained in other teachings. This was illustrated by the imagery of the wheel. At the periphery, the spokes of the wheel were most distant from one another. As one moved towards the center, the spokes gradually got closer and at the hub all spokes were united.

It is true that the religion one was born into was the best place for one to start one's spiritual development. However, it was not correct to think that the religion one was born into was the best religion in the world and that other religions were inferior.

In God's plan of action for fostering the spiritual development of all mankind, each religion was a separate chapter in God's big manual of guidance for the spiritual development of human beings. Each spiritual teacher sent to planet earth by God, whether he was called Prophet, Son of God, Avatar or teacher brought with him or her sufficient spiritual energy, divine blessings and love to be able to impart the teachings both by word and example. The time and place of birth of the teachers had deep meaning and significance.

In the philosophy of religion, syncretism means or conveys the idea that different religions, instead of being conflicting, are complementary to each other. I tend to agree with that view. God sent the teachers at the right time to the right places, to reveal a single syncretic master religion progressively revealed for the benefit of mankind, as in a book with several chapters.or installments in a correspondence course. This view is not new, as many spiritual teachings from the most ancient such as Kabbalah, to the more recent such as the Baha'i faith and Sathya Sai Baba of the present time strongly promulgate this view. Syncretism has also been the focal point of the teachings of Vedic Masters such as Sri Aurobindo, Ramakrishna and Ramana Maharshi who believed that the truth is one, but sages call it by different names. Monastic Christian writers such as Boehme and Merton have expressed this view in their writings. According to my view, there is One all powerful Supreme Divine Entity who may be called Brahman, God or such other name according to one's religion of birth or conviction. It (God) was saturated with only positive energies. It is a Positive Entity with no negative elements or energies corresponding to a Satan or a devil. If there is an evil power called Satan or devil, it also has to operates under the supremacy of omnipotent God. They may be comparable to the uniformed services of a government such as the army and police forces, who are allowed to use armaments and tools to inflict pain for the purpose of enforcing law and order under the control of a peace-loving government. Under no circumstance can any evil force exercise greater power than God.

The Internet is a present day divine blessing as it includes an incomparable collection of spiritual material to be used by anybody who is interested to find out about other spiritual teachings. This is a contrast from the distant past, when, to find out about another religious faith, one had to travel long distances, even risking one's life. Of course, the Internet is like a wild jungle with irresponsible websites, which could lead to confusion. But if used with discretion it could be a goldmine of knowledge. Discretion is necessary. A recommended sequence for exploration, based on my experience, would be as follows: First study one's own religion, including origins, historical backgrounds and comparative statistics of distribution in different parts of the world. Secondly, read old and new material about one's religion including authors with radical views. Thirdly, explore esoteric and alternative teachings relating to one's religion. Lastly, read basic material about other religions and alien practices that are prevalent in your present day society, e.g. ancient teachings about Yoga, Tai Chi, Fenshui, etc. In learning other religions and cultural systems, it is highly recommended to obtain guidance from someone who belongs to that culture. One has to be careful not to follow teachers who offer shortcuts and instant enlightenment, which could be similar to jumping in at the deep end of the bathing pool before learning to swim. Always start with the simple basics.

What I present in the following chapters are my own experiences in learning religious and spiritual paths. My experiences can be used as case studies, but I hesitate to recommend that anyone'should follow my footsteps blindly. What is right for one may not be right for another.

Sometimes when people ask me what religion I belong to, I jokingly reply, "buffet" What I mean is that we have access to many beautiful teachings, like in a smorgasbord with a wide spread of all types of food, where I am free to select what appeals to me as the most desirable at that particular time. At another time, I might select something else.

After having made detailed studies of different religions, my opinion is that they are not conflicting with one another. The role of divine messengers or Avatars is not only to correct errors, but more to guide and promote future growth. Because the divine messengers who brought them to the world spoke different languages and lived in different cultural environments at different times there are superficial differences that need intelligent interpretation and adjustment. While finding a perfect analogy is difficult, I would liken the process to a correspondence course on religion written by God himself, and sent to the world through his messengers. Each lesson gets crystallized as a different religion. If I say that I prefer lesson six to all other lessons and therefore will not bother to read the other lessons, I will not be able to make full use of the correspondence course and therefore will remain partially ignorant. We should not try to learn other religions merely for criticism, before making an adequate study of the religion one is born into. This should include the esoteric teachings associated with each religion if possible. Some examples are monastic Christianity, Mormon Christianity, Rosicrucian teachings and books such as St. John of the Cross for Christians, Mahayana, Zen and Vajrayana teachings for Theravada Buddhism and the Sufi teachings for Islam.

I am not asking all readers to follow my example, but this has been my guiding principle in devoting time and effort to learning other religions. I feel I have been amply rewarded. What concerned me most were my needs at that time. However, joining a local religious community could give immense social benefits, in addition to spiritual development. Some religious and self-development practices, which I found particularly beneficial in my life, are described below.

I remember my childhood as a Methodist when I never had an opportunity to examine the belief systems of even Baptists the faith to which many of my friends belonged. Hinduism and Buddhism were not even recognized as religions. My thirst for knowledge, fired by my illuminatory spiritual experience drove me to explore all those outside religions in secrecy hidden from the view of my parents and relations. I visited the Buddhist temples whenever I got a chance. I also enjoyed the beautiful devotional music in the Hindu temples, at bhajan ceremonies associated with ceremonies such as Vel.

Human life has unlimited potential which can be activated with the right knowledge, skills and effort. The parable of the airplane has been used to illustrate this fact. In this story the airplane is our body. During World War I a very small airplane was grounded in a remote community. After a long period, someone discovered the possibility of pushing it around on its wheels, and it came to be used by the villagers to transport heavy objects such as firewood. Still later a man who owned some cattle tethered two of them to the airplane and transformed it into a bullock cart. Long afterwards a licensed car driver discovered in it meters and switches similar to what he found in his car. He filled it with gas and managed to start the engine and drive short distances on the surface. Years later a trained aircraft pilot filled it with the appropriate fuel and oils and flew it away. The marvelous potential of the human body, described as having been created in the likeness of the Creator himself, is rarely made full use of. Not being aware of all its potential to fly, we underutilize the resources and use it as a car or a cart. This story illustrates the need to recognize and upgrade our talents and skills till we can use our own bodies and souls to the best advantage, through conscious self-development. It is not an easy task to write about all religious systems that I have come across in my life, in one book. My intention is to give readers some introductory material about a few religious systems I have come across and benefited from.

The simpler and popular levels of religion and spiritual development are the most common while the more advanced levels are understood and followed by only a few. The highest levels are not even known to exist by most religious practitioners. A good analogy is a pyramid where the lower levels are broader and spacious, but gets narrower and narrower with more limited space at higher levels. In the same way most people are content to stagnate at lower levels of mental and spiritual growth and remain at the base level while only a few exert the necessary effort to rise to higher levels of spiritual development.

As religions are different blends of the same or similar ingredients, they should lend themselves to a systematic codification of ideas. I was happy to see compendiums of spiritual teachings such as Aldous Huxley's Perennial Philosophy and Huston Smith's "World's Religions, Our Great Wisdom Traditions". The on-line Essays in the History of Religions by Joachim Bach with about

5000 excellent articles is a vast reference source for those interested. However in my opinion we need more detailed and sophisticated data indexes and codifications covering all religions without any bias. The Encyclopedia of Religion by Mircea Eliade is an excellent contribution.

Chapter 6

Hinduism A Living Cosmos

Hinduism has its origin in one of the most ancient sets of scriptures called the Vedas dating back to about 4000 years. It treats the entire cosmos as a living being and integrates all its functions and components in a systemic theological hierarchy. Brahman is at the top of the divine hierarchy. At the next lower level there are three major deities comparable with the three main functional systems of a living being i.e. (i.) Brahma is the maintainer of life energy and creator of new life. (ii.) Vishnu is the sustainer or repository of life energy and is in charge of the maintenance of life in the entire cosmos, and (iii.) Shiva represents the utilization of life energy for the entire complex of life activity, and is called the Lord of the Cosmic Dance. Each of the large number of other deities represents a different aspect or function of the cosmic life system. For example, the three supreme deities are supported in their functions by their consorts. i. Saraswathi, goddess of knowledge supports Brahma in his functions of creation and evolution, ii. Lakshmi, goddess of wealth and physical resources assists Vishnu in his functions of preservation and maintenance of the cosmos, and iii. Shakti, goddess of energy assists Shiva, who activates and balances all cosmic movements. One of the most important functions of Vishnu, is that of sending his incarnations or avatars at appropriate times for the preservation of righteous life by reinforcing the energies that stand for good. According to this view all founders of world religions are avatars of Vishnu. All divine functions, each represented by a deity, are further subdivided into a vast array of divine entities, of which one may be selected by each devotee or group of devotees to be the center of devotion. Ultimately, it is the one'supreme God who is thus symbolized in so many forms, each with a different name and physical attributes.

Vishnu and Shiva as well as their consorts are the most worshipped of Hindu gods. Brahma is not generally an object of worship. For almost every deity there are stories that assert the supremacy of that deity. This concept is called henotheism, according to which the deity one worships is regarded as the supreme reality. Yoga, which is one of the principal forms in which Hinduism is practiced, has a number of divisions according to the focus of attention, e.g. Hatha yoga for physical development, Jnana Yoga for mental development, Bhakti Yoga for devotional upliftment and Raja Yoga for spiritual development, which includes meditation and the activation of Kundalini energy through the seven chakras or spiritual centers. I am in total agreement with Sri Aurobindo, who believed that the entire cosmos is a living entity, with all living beings functioning as its cells. Through the practice of Yoga we assist in the further evolution of ourselves, as well as this totality, towards Satchitananda (Sat =right being, Chit=right consciousness and Ananda=absolute bliss), and achieving this state of inner joy as the primary purpose of human and all life.

Chapter 7

Buddhism The Four Noble Truths

The question Why I Live? had a special significance for Prince Siddhartha of India, who in the sixth century before Christ, left his palace determined to find an answer to the enigma of life, typified by the phenomena of old age, sickness, death and renunciation. He contemplated on the implications and nature of human life and meditated till he found the right answers and then preached for forty-five years as Lord Buddha. In his first sermon he summarized his teachings in the Four Noble Truths, which provided a universally valid strategy for solving any problem situation such as continued human suffering. The first truth or step in the annihilation of suffering was concentrating on the present problem situation and identifying the imperfections. The second step was the analysis of the problem situation with a view to ascertaining the reasons or causes that led to the imperfections. The third requirement was to formulate in your mind the perfect state that one desired to achieve, free from all imperfections. The fourth and final step was the formulation of a strategy and an action plan for achieving the final goal. The Noble Eightfold Path was an enumeration of the eight steps that were required for achieving the goal of life, which was the annihilation of human suffering. In the Eightfold Path the first six steps were behavioral, namely right worldview, right intention, right speech, right action, right livelihood, and right effort. The seventh crucial requirement was cultivating concentration and self-remembering at all times. Meditation was the ultimate step. These steps were amply elaborated in his teachings, which were contained in the Tripitaka (three baskets) containing the three main divisions of his teachings, namely the text, disciplinary stipulations and advanced expositions.

The main goal of Buddhism was the elimination of suffering to reveal the natural tranquility of life, which is called Nirvana. If one desires to obtain a deeper and broader understanding of Buddhism, it is necessary to study and practice its esoteric paths, particularly Zen (Mahayana) Buddhism of Japan with its focus in meditation, and the Vajrayana tradition of Tibetan Buddhism which focuses on the generation and utilization of subtle energies through higher meditations, chants, initiations and ceremonies.

Chapter 8

Christianity Path to Salvation

Christianity is based on the teachings of Jesus Christ who was born at the beginning of the Christian era. Speaking as the Son of God, he preached the word of God and demonstrated it through acts of brotherly love and selfless service. When asked what was the most important of all the commandments or rules Jesus replied that you should love God with all your heart and mind and strength and also love your neighbor as you love yourself. (Mark 12:31) This is called the golden rule of Christianity.

I was born to a Christian family and was brought up under all its good influences, through Sunday schools, Wesley Guilds and participation in community service programs. My parents believed in daily family prayer at which each of us took turns to offer prayers. What appealed to me most in early childhood was the concept of an omnipotent, omniscient and omnipresent God, in whom you can trust and who loved you personally, and to whom one could pray directly. I am deeply thankful for all the good that Christianity has done for me and is doing for the world then and now. As basic information about the Bible and Christianity is readily available I do not intend highlighting any elements of Christianity. It is not possible to make an accurate and comprehensive summary of Christian teaching and call it Christianity, not only because there are many different versions of the doctrine, but also because, according to Christian doctrine, the essence of Christianity includes both the word and the spirit of Jesus Christ as Savior. It was quite some time later that I discovered Monastic Christianity, and was surprised to see how only very few Christians read these fascinating writings. I differed from normal Christian practice only in one respect for which I could be grateful to God almighty; this is my great desire to learn other faiths. In Western Christianity, we have a reluctance, almost a fear, of exploring spiritual practices related to other religions. This aversion comes from priestly admonitions that invoke in us a fear that if we expose ourselves to other teachings, we will in some subtle way diminish the strength of our own religious tradition. Those who practiced monastic religion preserved to a great extent the simplicity and spiritual depth of the teachings of Christ, as is illustrated by Philokalia, the best known collection of Monastic Christian writings. The Philokalia is a collection of text written between the fourth and fifteenth centuries by spiritual masters of the Orthodox Christian tradition. These were first published in Greek in 1782, translated into Slavonic and later into Russian. The Philokalia has exercised an influence far greater than that of any book other than the Bible in the recent history of the Orthodox Church. Thomas Merton, a well-known Christian monk, did not limit his spiritual practices to those of Western Christianity. He explored the practices of the East and found that the manifestation of God in his own life was not limited to the spiritual practices that were a part of his own monastic Christian tradition.

Chapter 9

Islam

Islam is a major world religion founded in Arabia in the 7th century AD by Muhammad (570AD to 632AD). He became a spiritual teacher after receiving a powerful spiritual revelation in his fortieth year. (610AD) From very early times, Muslim traders sailed to Eastern countries like Sri Lanka to collect spices, gems and other merchandise to be taken to European countries. Some Arabs settled down in these countries so that there was a considerable Muslim population in my country. When I was still a child, we had a Muslim family as neighbors. They were very friendly and we were always invited to their feasts, where food was plentiful and delicious. The chants too were very melodious and peaceful. Food and money were freely distributed at these festivals. We were impressed by their great concern for following their religious tenets very strictly, such as praying five times a day. Still later when I worked for over 3 years in Morocco I had more direct contact with Islamic society, culture and religion. Some highly educated Europeans whom I came to know in Morocco were deeply interested in Sufism and through them I did considerable reading of books on Islam.

The Five Pillars of Islam sum up the religious obligations of all Muslims.

1. Acceptance of Allah as the only God, and Muhammad as the only messenger of Allah.
2. Salat or observation of Prayer.
3. Zakat or Alms giving
4. Hajj or Pilgrimage to the House of Allah.
5. Bukhari or observation of fasting during Ramadhan

The fundamental faith in Islam is the Sharia, or Law, which embraces the way of life as commanded by God. They pray five times a day and engage themselves in community worship on Fridays at the mosque, where an imam leads the service of worship. All believers are required to make a pilgrimage to Mecca, at least once in a lifetime, barring excusable obstacles such as poverty or sickness. During our three-year stay in Morocco in the seventies, we had direct experience of how rigidly the fasting and all requirements of religious worship were observed. City life which was almost dead during Ramadhan at day time came back alive at night when jubilant crowds in colorful togas and long shirts walked up and down the streets partaking of different kinds of sweetmeats and drinking scented sherberts. Vigorous drum beats from the belly-dancing booths added to the carnival spirit. Alcohol and pork were not allowed to be consumed in any Islamic household. Gambling, usury, fraud, slander, and the making of images were forbidden. The other obligatory celebrations were Muhammad's birthday (mawlid) and his ascension into heaven (miraj).

Chapter 10

Gurdjieff & Ouspensky Waking up from sleep

In my third year at the University in 1947, I selected a three year specialized program in History, culture and Oriental Languages. It was directly under the Dean of the Faculty, Professor Ratnasuriya. I developed a great liking to him and always felt that his seminars had an inner quality that I did not see in others. At that time I had a deep yearning for furthering my spiritual knowledge and was experimenting different avenues. As a teenager, I came across a shack by the side of the road in which sat a very old man selling secondhand books. On my selecting a very old copy of "Rosicrucian Cosmo-conception" the old man looked at me closely. He asked me why I wanted that book and whether I was really interested in reading it. I told him that I like to read books of all types and particularly any books on spiritual development. He muttered that I may be too young to read it. Having read parts of that book, I decided to explore those teachings further. When much later I came across some material on the Rosicrucian Movement at the University library, I requested for more information from USA. At that time even the airmail postage was a big slice off my limited pocket money. I was thrilled when the big packet from USA arrived at last, but was frustrated to learn that the amount I had to pay was far beyond my means. I also was not sure whether it was exactly what I needed. It was at this stage that I thought of seeking advice from Professor Ratnasuriya. He welcomed me in his office and saw the package of Rosicrucian papers. With a look of surprise, he said "I had no idea that you were interested in this kind of study". To my surprise he invited me to his house the following Wednesday evening. It was the beginning of a new Gurdjieff group. I felt I was so lucky as I was the only University student he had invited. This was indeed a very important stage in my spiritual journey. I felt I had been selected to join Gurdjieff work by some higher intelligence and made a determination to continue attending group work. Something that made me to continue with Gurdjieff work was the realization that these teachings were very similar to what I received in my seventh year illumination. I was immensely excited to notice the unmistakable identity of the model and was delighted that at last I was beginning to find material that collaborated the knowledge I received in my childhood revelatory experience.

The Gurdjieff and Ouspensky movement which I joined around 1949 at the age of 21 through my University teacher and guru Professor Ratnasuriya had its focus on developing self-awareness and self-remembering. We had weekly group meetings for work at which there were different exercises to ensure constant attention on ourselves. It was emphasized that we need to be constantly aware of ourselves. Normally our attention is like an arrow pointing outwards with no self-awareness, whereas, ideally, the arrow of attention should be double pointed, one pointing outwards and the other inwards. The related exercises, although difficult, were extremely interesting and beneficial. More advanced groups used dance movements to the accompaniment of especially composed music. I practiced the exercises with all enthusiasm and with a clear understanding that I had received this guidance from the highest level of omniscience. Attending the "work" sessions was my most joyful activity at that time. Gurdjieff taught that most human beings are not fully awake, but pretended to be so. They were like the prisoners in Plato's cave. The purpose of his work was to restore work participants to full consciousness so that they could work towards their own development. The main tool for restoring those who are sleeping to full consciousness was constant Self-remembering. From his young days, Gurdjieff (1879-1949) undertook hazardous journeys to different parts of the world searching for hidden knowledge. Gurdjieff's journeys are the subject of a fascinating book "Meetings with Remarkable Men" and a movie of the book under the same name, directed by Peter Brook. Gurdjieff called his system of inner growth The Fourth Way, claiming that it transcended the three traditional spiritual paths of the monk, the yogi, and the fakir. He taught that it is possible to live The Fourth Way while still living in the world without having to lead a socially isolated life in a community of like-minded seekers. We were saddened by the news of Gurdjieff's death in 1949 but the group work continued and used Xerox copies of lessons received from Ouspensky, who continued Gurdjieff's work. Gurdjieff, described the cosmic energy distribution process as the Ray of Creation. He taught how the vivifying spectrum of energies, both psychic and physical, as are appropriate and needed for each of the seven levels of the holarchy were emanated and flowed from the highest level of the Creator, through each of the lower levels of life for life maintenance and activating spiritual growth at each level. Thus the sun supplies all innumerable physical energy needs of our planet such as food, fuel, heat, light and energy directly or indirectly. All carbohydrates needed for life maintenance by living beings on earth are manufactured in the leaves or other green parts of vegetables through photosynthesis, by the combination of sunlight and carbon dioxide with chlorophyll as the catalyst. This pattern repeats itself at all levels. The sun in turn receives its energy from the galaxy, which acquires it from the highest level of the creator. The godhead in this way sustains the psychic and physical energy needs of the entire universe. As it is difficult to summarize or even enumerate all aspects of Gurdjieff teachings in this introduction, I refer interested readers to suggested reading and online websites.

Chapter II

Subud Guidance to Find the Right Path

In 1958 I was working for the Sri Lanka government in the district of Matara, when the Ceylon Observer, the most popular English Newspaper of the Country carried a full-page book review written by Tarzie Vittachi, the most famous English journalist of the country, about J.G.Bennett's book Concerning Subud. I knew of J.G. Bennett as the world-coordinator of the Gurdjieff movement of which I was a member. I knew this must have been an extraordinary book for being reviewed by Tarzie himself and ordered it immediately. I had heard that before Gurdjieff's death he had advised his followers to be watchful for a teacher from the East who would continue Gurdjieff's work. Concerning Subud was one of the most fascinating books I had read and was determined to join the movement even before finishing the book. I found the address of the Subud center in Colombo, and wrote that I would like to come to the center to join the group. I received a reply quite promptly with an invitation to the center in Colombo giving route details. It was mentioned that a member could attend two latihans (this word means exercise in Indonesian) per week. Because there were two latihans on Sundays I planned to go on Sundays to attend both latihans.

The following Sunday I drove the hundred miles from Matara to Colombo and found the large building where I met several of my friends, including some who were members of the Gurdjieff movement. We were told that normally there was a waiting period of one to three months, but this requirement had been suspended because ours was a new group. I was extremely happy to hear that, because I was impatient to experience the energy of Subud which Bennett had described so graphically. As we walked upstairs and entered the door of the latihan room, I had strange feelings with a marked fear of the unknown. I stood still and tried to calm my mind, which became impossible as the whole crowd filled the room and started moving in all directions while uttering unusual sounds. I later discovered that only a small section of the group made most of the movements and the sounds, while others engaged themselves in calmer movements in relative silence. After the second latihan in the evening I headed for home. I felt an inner peace and tranquility of mind which was quite unusual for me.

The Subud movement started in Indonesia in the mid twenties, when a young man called Muhammad Subuh received an enlightenment. He saw and felt a large ball of light entering his body generating strong inner vibrations. This experience, which repeated itself many times, transformed his body and soul. He gradually realized that this experience came from God the Almighty for the purpose of transforming human society by making it easy for man to find out the Will of God, and also that it could be transmitted easily to anyone who desired it sincerely. Subud is not a teaching, not a belief, not even a practice. It is a receiving and can be properly understood only through experience. The word Subud is an abbreviation of three words, Susila (right living according to the will of God), Buddhi (a human faculty for receiving divine communications for our guidance) and Dharma (the divine source of guidance, which may be understood to be God). When one opens oneself to the divine source of vibrations emanating from the highest levels, this energy can be used, to develop sensitivity to the spiritual energy and receive divine guidance. The process of receiving is called latihan, which in Indonesian means exercise. At the beginning latihans are held in groups. After the inner energies are well established, one can practice latihan individually, after obtaining permission from the senior members, called helpers. Later this spiritual energy can be used for obtaining guidance through life, by a process called testing, in which the question is brought to your mind while in a state of latihan. The subtle energy manifestations are observed while testing as they help to convey the answers to the questions. It is difficult to explain the process clearly in words, but I found the process quite easy to practice, and received guidance in a most miraculous fashion. Submission, surrender, sincerity and patience are the four key words given by the founder for the guidance of members.

While we were living in Badulla, my father-in-law found the windy weather too cold for his asthmatic condition and desired to spend the night at a hotel in the hill station of Bandarawela. When I took him there I met a person at the hotel who saw a Subud publication in my hand and started criticizing the Subud movement. I found him to be educated and well-read. He argued that when you left open your inner mind to Subud, even evil forces could enter your system and thus cause harm. He said he knew a number of such cases. While driving back home to Badulla, I was somewhat disturbed by his stories. That night I did latihan alone in my office room and library, where I had many bookracks containing nearly thousand books on many subjects. During latihan I moved round and round till I lost my bearings and walked towards the wall and touched a bookrack, and took a book out and turned to a page all with my eyes closed. I kept the page open and switched on the light, and read the page. It was page 191 of A.C.Bouquet's "Sacred Books of the World", Pelican Edition, describing the call of Moses mentioned in Exodus iii. 1-6 & 12-14. I read the paragraph where I had put my finger. It read "And Moses said unto God, Behold, when I come unto the children of Israel, and shall say unto them, The God of your fathers hath sent me unto you; and they shall say to me, What is His name? What shall I say unto them? And God said unto Moses, I AM THAT I AM and he said, "Thus shalt thou say unto the children of Israel, I AM hath sent me unto you. "The book went on to quote some poems inspired by the story of this theophany, for example: "No pebbles at your feet but proves a sphere. No chaffinch but implies the cherubim, Earth's crammed with Heaven, and every common bush Afire with God. But only he sees it who takes off his shoes The rest sit round and pluck blackberries." I was astonished at the relevance of the imagery. It was an unmistakable confirmation that the power I had contacted in Subud latihan is no other than that of Almighty God. All my doubts vanished into thin air. I had numerous incidents of this nature associated with Subud practice, which made it immensely clear that the power of Subud originated from the highest spiritual level. Bapak wrote a book called Susila Buddhi Dharma, which he said was received from God to explain the origin and nature of Subud. The following extracts from the book explain the conditions under which human beings can receive contact with the Great Life, whose source is in fact the Power of God Almighty. "God is powerful and far excels man in all things; for in very truth He is the Creator of mankind and of heaven and earth. So man as he really is, then, is just a created thing, powerless before God. Necessarily, since this is his real condition, man cannot with his heart and mind understand or reflect on the Nature and Power of God. So man, in seeking the nature of worship that can make contact with the Great Life, needs above all to stop the welling up of his imagination and thinking. For by doing that he really paralyses his nafsu (passions) and surrenders his human ability and wisdom; that is to say, the human being obeys and submits with complete sincerity to God who rules within him. This in fact is nothing new, for men of old followed this path and found a contact of this quality that they could feel within them. Why, then, are there not many people like that in our own times that still have that contact? The reason is simply that conditions on earth for mankind keep changing as generation succeeds generation, and many people are easily affected by the influence of these ever-changing conditions that face them. Especially has this been so as the human mind has progressively developed its science. This has, as it were, increasingly opened the way for the inner feeling to fall from the realm of inner peace into the realm of thought. In consequence, the human self gradually comes to be ruled more and more by thought, instead of by the quietness of the inner feeling or the inner self, so that in the end man's emotions and brain are always busy and his inner feeling has almost no opportunity to be at peace. Certainly men must think, for thought is an important tool with which they can strive to fulfill the needs of their life on earth and so make their existence here an orderly one. But to become aware of the spiritual life [kejiwaan] and make contact a gain with the Great Life men do not need to use their minds. On the contrary, they should stop the process of their thinking and imagining. For only by so doing can a person receive something from beyond his reach that at length attracts a vibration of energy felt within the self. Clearly, then, the sole way to make contact with the Great Life, or with the Power of God, is for a man to surrender sincerely and earnestly. And this surrender must not be in word only, but must penetrate throughout his inner feeling until he truly feels that he believes in, praises and worships no one but God Almighty. This truth was often stated by those who received while living on earth in centuries long past. They said that man's one and only way to be able to draw near to the Power of God is that he must be willing to quieten his inner feeling with complete patience, trust and sincerity. This has been an absolute requirement, for in truth this gift from God can only be received by those who have inner feelings filled with surrender, patience, trust and sincerity before the Greatness of God.

Chapter 12

Sathya Sai Baba

Sathya Sai Baba, a contemporary spiritual teacher in Southern India is worthy of special mention, not only for the unprecedented following from all parts of the world, but also for the nature of his teaching and achievements. I have visited his ashram and have personally felt a divine presence. He started demonstrating supernatural powers at an early age and was declared a divine avatar. He has attracted devotees from most religions and nationalities from the West and other parts of the world, and has emerged as a spiritual teacher of a very high order. In addition to his daily talks, he performs countless miracles of all types, which he says are only his visiting cards. He encourages the study and practice of all major religions and hosts their religious functions in his Ashram without any exception. The ability to do this in a country where religious strife is rampant is by itself a miracle. He has transformed the rural hamlet of Puttaparthy where he lives, into an exemplary township, with advanced community services, primary, secondary and university education, an airport, specialized medical facilities and, particularly a hospital providing advanced heart surgery, which is absolutely free to anybody who comes there. When I went there with my wife we searched for a donation box, which is a common practice in Indian ashrams, or rather any place of religious worship in the world. There were none. Ultimately we had to take the donation to the office, where we were given a receipt for the amount donated. I consider it a great blessing that a divine teacher of this caliber is living amongst us today. I give below some of his sayings: "All religions are roads leading to the one and the only goal, that is God. So regard them all with equal respect. All religions teach that you should purify your mind, know your own self and develop Love. Silence is the only language of the realized. It is only in the depth of silence that the voice of God can be heard. Silence stills the waves of one's heart. All rivers merge with the ocean. Similarly all creation and all streams of life merge with the Source, namely God. Aspire for that happy consummation.

Chapter 13

Some Other Spiritual Paths

As there are innumerable self-development and spiritual paths in the world today, it is not possible to assess them or prioritize them using any external criteria. I believe that when one achieves a sufficient degree of sensitivity to the spiritual energies through personal effort, he or she is led to the right people and places required for further growth. I have been very fortunate in my life to be brought in contact with the paths that were suitable for me, and I have mentioned them in this book. What I write here are my own experiences and their suitability for the reader has to be personally determined. This is the reason why esoteric teachings are kept hidden. For example a fourth grader cannot understand degree level mathematics. Sincerity and patience have to be cultivated, with some degree of surrender to higher intelligence to guide one on the right path. I give below very short introductory notes about a few of the other paths, which I have come to know through personal contacts. The esoteric paths connected with major religions have to be treated as separate paths because they have got separated and are found to be operating as independent organizations. I bless all spiritual seekers and their ventures.

Monastic and Mystical Christianity

Many devout Christians have sought to separate themselves from church organizations so that they could practice their spiritual development activities in relative solitude. I myself have always preferred solitary prayer and meditation for experiencing higher consciousness. I know that experiences of higher consciousness are achieved not by mental effort, but by quieting the world of senses. However extreme caution is required about seeking and following new spiritual paths. The best way to understand such less known paths is to read a book by or study the life of one of their followers. A few of them I am conversant with are St Ignatius, St John of the Cross (John Yepes), St Teresa, Jacob Boehme and Hildegard von Bingen. Many mystical Christian writings that are not well known are found in the Philokalia. This is a collection of text written between the fourth and fifteenth centuries by Christian spiritual masters of the Orthodox tradition. It is recognized as having exercised an influence far greater than that of any book other than the Bible, in the recent history of the Orthodox Church.

Sufism

Sufism is the best-known mystical movement within Islam that seeks to find divine love and knowledge through direct personal experience of God. Sufi practitioners have often been at odds with the mainstream of Islamic theology and law. They devised many practices that help to loosen the bonds of the lower self, enabling the soul to experience the higher reality toward which it naturally aspires. For this purpose some well known Sufis left their homes for extended periods to live the difficult life of a mendicant carrying nothing but a thick beggar's robe. I was able to learn about sufi ritual and read some of their less-known biographical writings through a British Subud member I met in Morocco who had close contacts with Sufis, and attende d Sufi group meetings. The importance of Sufism in the history of Islam is incalculable and Sufi love poetry, as those of Rumi, represent a golden age in Middle Eastern literature.

Baha'i

Baha'i faith is worthy of special mention because it is in perfect agreement with my thinking about the ideal of religious harmony and measures needed to implement such changes. Baha ullah founded the movement in Iran 150 years ago. The main Bahai teaching is that there is only one God and that God is actively concerned about the development of humanity. He taught about the oneness of religion and that divine messengers such as Abraham, Moses, Zoroaster, Krishna, Buddha, Christ, Muhammad, Bab and Baha ullah were given to humanity to educate people in morals and in social values including the oneness of humanity and the unity of all religions. The Bab who was born in Iran in 1819 announced in 1844 that he was the promised teacher or Mahdi expected by Muslims. The Baha'i scriptures constitute the books, essays, and letters composed by these two teachers.

The Baha'i brotherhood is an independent world religion and has spread widely in 232 countries. During my ten-year period of work in Botswana I was associated with a Baha'i community who were playing an active role in bringing together the various racial and religious communities in that country. I was greatly impressed by their services and enthusiasm. After analyzing the challenges facing humanity, the Baha'i teachings have been formulated suggesting the acceptance of moral and spiritual principles, which have been summarized by Shoghi Effendi, the head of the Baha'i Faith from 1921 to 1957 as follows: "The unity of the human race, as envisaged by Baha'ullah, implies the establishment of a world commonwealth in which all nations, races, creeds and classes are closely and permanently united, and in which the autonomy of its state members and the personal freedom and initiative of the individuals that compose them are definitely and completely safeguarded. This commonwealth must, as far as we can visualize it, consist of a world legislature, whose members will, as the trustees of the whole of mankind, ultimately control the entire resource of all the component nations, and will enact such laws as shall be required to regulate the life, satisfy the needs and adjust the relationships of all races and peoples. In such a world society, science and religion, the two most potent forces in human life, will be reconciled, will cooperate, and will harmoniously develop."

Some more paths, which had attracted my attention and may appeal to some readers for exploration are I Ching, Kabbalah, Tantra, Zen, Tibetan Buddhism, Astrology, and Huna teachings of Hawaai. I might write about them if and when I get further opportunities to discuss them.

PART THREE

MY SPIRITUAL EXPERIENCES

IIIA Introductory

I have had several spiritual experiences that I consider to be landmarks in the spiritual development process of my life. Some of the most important of those experiences are described in this Section. These experiences have a common theme in that they concern the working of subtle energies outside the normal physical and mental faculties. Cosmic consciousness experiences make sense only to those who have had some experience or understanding of the subtle bodies, which are made up of finer energies that are beyond the reach of scientists and medical doctors. These experiences, demonstrate the interactions that take place within energy systems forming networks that interact among different levels of cosmic life, enabling the transmission of energies, intelligence and knowledge across time and space. Chakra activations and Near Death Experiences provide additional evidence of such life-transforming occurrences. I could relate these experiences to my worldview that the cosmos is a living entity and that human beings are living cells of the cosmos, which like battery cells containing electricity, are distributed throughout the body enabling the working of different functional systems and organs within the body. There are concealed patterns of distribution and communication of cosmic energy, for which different names such as chi, kundalini, shakti, etc. are used in yogic and tantric literature. It is only through a proper synthesis of Eastern and Western perspectives that personal experiences involving such energies could be properly studied and understood. Details of personal experiences as I have given below may be used as case studies in such studies.

Chapter 14

My Experience of Cosmic Consciousness

My Cosmic Consciousness experience, which took place in my seventh year, was the most significant and outstanding spiritual experience in my whole life. Its influence and impact has been felt in all fields and aspects of my life during my entire lifespan. It set in motion a holistic spiritual growth process, giving me abundant power, knowledge, guidance and joy that manifested during all stages of my life. I cannot think of any important activity in my life thereafter, which had not been influenced by this experience in a very substantial manner. It is strange that I have not known the words cosmic consciousness and other words that I have used to describe the experience till long after the experience, mostly through my readings and studies in metaphysics. Looking back at those experiences in retrospect, I see it as the beginning of an inner process within me, comparable to the germination of a seed, the conception of a new life or consciousness of direct participation in the continuous process of cosmic creation. Even when I am not consciously thinking of it, I am constantly aware of its dynamic inner working bringing forth creativity, intelligence, and psychic energy. Its benefits manifest continuously as a process of constant growth that is guided by Higher Intelligence. I felt an inner urge to share my experience with everybody by writing this book, because I realized the value of first hand autobiographical narratives, which are needed to provide valid data for understanding and authenticating mystical experiences of this type. However to do this I had to overcome a number of enormous psychological obstacles. After the initial problems encountered by me in the process of communicating the experience to my father and others close to me, I had promised myself not to talk about it to anybody till I have found independent scientific evidence to validate my experience and revelations. I was also conscious of the need to explain not only what happened outside of me, but also what changes occurred inside of me, in the innermost recesses of my mind and soul. In narrating intimate personal experiences, which cannot be validated through any other means, I had to be absolutely honest with utmost concern for accuracy while carrying out this task. I appeal to the readers to depend on their inner sensibility when reading this material, as much as I had been in my communication. As I had no intentions of writing about this particular experience I did not have to worry about giving this experience a specific name. I simply called it my experience. The question of giving it a name came up only when I decided to write this book. The word cosmic consciousness that the Canadian psychologist Richard M Bucke used in his classic on the subject seemed to be the best available, as I could see that my experience was very similar to what he described as Cosmic Consciousness. I thought of the word Epiphany but was reluctant to use it because of its biblical associations. So it is with some reservations that I chose the word cosmic consciousness.

The event is still fresh in my memory, as if it happened only yesterday. It was a beautiful sunny morning. I was spending my Easter school vacation in my mother's ancestral home and garden in a village area close to the town of Negombo in Sri Lanka. A large garden full of flower bushes and fruit trees surrounded the house. There were also some cinnamon trees and coconut palms. A thick carpet of grass, mixed with many smaller plants and weeds, covered the ground, as the garden had not been tidied for sometime. I was walking through the garden by myself as I used to do quite often. I knew every inch of this garden. Small carnivorous plants growing close to the ground that trap small ants and insects attracted me, as I enjoyed setting free the small insects trapped in them. While I was walking by a cinnamon tree, I stopped to examine a cinnamon leaf that had a brownish patch on it. I touched the leaf and noticed the intricate network of veins under it, which I recognized as an unmistakable sign of life. I remember wondering whether the tree was conscious of my presence. Then, I became aware of something strange happening around me and also within me including a difference in my perception of the outside world. The light surrounding me changed to a golden hue and became brighter as it engulfed me. I had a feeling of calm and joy. I felt perfect peace in my mind with a sensation that my body was becoming expanded and weightless. My normal thinking process seemed to undergo a change. I find it impossible to describe accurately what my body and mind went through at that time, although I was fully conscious throughout this period. I seemed to feel I was larger in size than my normal self, even as tall as the trees. I felt the presence of a powerful source of energy, which empowered me. I also felt connected to a supreme intelligence giving me knowledge that I never possessed before.

After some time, I realized that the golden light was no more. Everything appeared to be normal once again. I was still standing alone near the cinnamon tree. The sudden and unexpected experiences made me feel somewhat strange. I had no trace of fear and felt quite calm inside, with an intense feeling of happiness. It was a totally blissful state. My mind was perfectly still with no outside thoughts, as if it had been washed clean. I was filled with abundant love and attachment towards everybody and everything as if I had discovered a new relationship to everything. The garden appeared to me as being more colorful and bright. I enjoyed this state of ecstasy for a while without moving away from the place. I realized that I have been given a new understanding that everything I saw around me was fully alive; animals, trees and plants and even rocks and sand. There was no place for hierarchy as each entity was of equal importance. Human beings could no longer be considered superior. Each entity was also in perpetual communication with all others. The most remarkable insight was that all entities, whether human, animal, vegetable or mineral was made of the very same relatively small particle, or basic building block. This entity, which was the smallest of all, was fully alive and served as the common building block within everything that existed. This brought into my mind Lego sets and pieces, which can be assembled in different ways to produce larger blocks of different shapes which can be reassembled further to form still larger shapes ad infinitum, with the difference that Lego pieces were not alive. According to my new experience and revelation, I realized that while the primary particle itself is alive, all the secondary and larger units and modules, which were built up by different conglomerations of these particles, whether small or large, were also fully alive, with feeling, intelligence and divine presence. Love was the glue that bound them all together. I myself too was a living part of this live cosmos.

As soon as I reached home I went to my father. My only problem at that time was about communicating my experience and the new revelations to him. He felt my excitement and asked me to tell him what it was all about. I found it difficult to give any coherent explanation. I tried to explain to him that I experienced that everything in the world, minerals, plants, animals and human beings, were made of one basic element, which was alive. He listened patiently and told me that according to his studies in science during his three-year science course in the college of teacher training from where he graduated, there were different atoms and molecules, which assembled to form different types of material. Therefore it was difficult for him to accept that all forms of matter were constituted of one's single type of element. He concluded that I had fallen asleep under the tree and had a dream. He advised me to take a good rest and try to forget it all. I was so disappointed with his response that I decided for myself not to discuss my experience with anybody at home.

The main elements of the experience can be summed up as follows

1. Everything in our universe, however large or small is both fully alive and fully conscious. This will include a human being, an ape, an ant, a rock and even a grain of sand.
2. All these entities are made of a common small life particle or building block, which is fully alive and conscious.
3. Every live particle and living being is in constant communication with all other living entities. This is a mind-boggling reality.
4. Love is omnipresent and is the glue that binds them all.

5. We, as all other living beings, are cells in the body of the cosmos, which is the ultimate reality, which we may call God in combination with the divine attributes of omnipotence, omniscience, omnipresence and omni-loving. All that we need to experience our unity with the cosmos or God is to increase our awareness to the fullest limit, sufficient enough to realize the truth.

6. The purpose of this entire life process, in which all entities from the cosmos and universe to the atoms and particles are participating, is the perpetual continuation of the cosmic growth process, which has many dimensions not accessible to us.

As explained in the first chapter, one of the most significant areas of impact of the Experience on my outside life was related to education. Without any doubt my intelligence and desire to learn got a heavy boost by my experience. My school test results and reports demonstrated this in no uncertain manner. When my father found my renewed interest in education and my high grades in schoolwork, he planned to send me to a higher level English School despite the additional expenditure. He knew a teacher in the selected English School who agreed to keep me in his home as a paying guest and who also undertook to supervise my studies. This led to a great improvement to my progress in schoolwork. The teacher was an avid reader and brought books home from the school library. Very often I finished reading them before he did. I completed my Senior School Certificate, a Government conducted Examination which was the highest class in that school, in my thirteenth year. Thereafter I joined Holy Cross College in Kalutara for my Higher School Certificate and University Entrance classes. I made good use of the more advanced library in this school, which had a full set of the latest Encyclopedia Britannica, which I always loved to read. This is where I read about Einstein's vain efforts to find positive proof of a Unified Field Theory. I gathered useful material in different fields of knowledge, even outside the prescribed syllabus, which helped me immensely in my higher examinations. I passed both the Higher School Certificate and the University Entrance Examination together, to the great satisfaction of my parents, and was ready to join the University in my seventeenth year. I was one of the youngest undergraduates, still unshaven, which made me the victim of severe senior ragging. I was not worried as I knew that I performed even better than the more elderly students in the classrooms and tests. I devoted an equal part of my time to reading religious scriptures, mostly of Hinduism and Buddhism, as I did not have sufficient access to them earlier. I had a great desire to learn all religious systems. Perhaps I overdid this, as I failed my First University Examination. This to me was an unimaginable catastrophe, for a number of reasons. This was the first and the last time I failed any examination, and caused me mental stress. It meant the duplication of one year's university education costs. What scared me most was the rule that if one failed the examination twice you had to leave the University. I decided to concentrate strictly on my syllabus at least for the time being and was successful in all the subsequent examinations.

The impact of the Cosmic Consciousness Experience on my mental and spiritual life has been profound and deep. I found it difficult to find words to describe the experience and its impact on my worldview. The words holon and holarchy coined by Arthur Koestler and popularized by authors such as Ken Wilbur seemed to satisfy my need for a word to describe my world view, and I started to use them in my writings. One of the words I used previously for this pattern of relationship was organic, because the anatomy of organisms, the relationship patterns of cells, tissues, organs with the circulatory and nervous systems impressed me as a good model of my vision of the cosmos.

Another word I used was systemic, because in my management studies I was impressed by the similarity of systemic structures to the pattern of relationships I wished to describe. This area of study was called Systems Thinking or Systems Theory. But for now, the terms holons and holarchy became my favorites, although I know that no terminology can provide a key to the perfect understanding of the knowledge that I received.

When I read much later the following paragraph from Bucke's classic treatise Cosmic Consciousness, I could not agree with him more fully, as what he described agreed with my experience so exactly. "The person who passes through this experience (of cosmic consciousness) will learn in the few minutes, or even moments, of its continuance more than in months or years of study, and he will learn much that no study ever taught or can teach. Especially does he obtain such a conception of THE WHOLE, or at least of an immense WHOLE, as dwarfs all conception, imagination or speculation, springing from and belonging to ordinary self consciousness, such a conception as makes the old attempts to mentally grasp the universe and its meaning petty and even ridiculous."

Chapter 15

Chakra Activation

I started experiencing chakra activation in meditation while I was working in Botswana in Southern Africa from 1979 to 1989. Since then I have had Kundalini energy manifestations whenever I meditated properly. I am certain that my seven year Cosmic Consciousness Experience had a direct impact by way of facilitating my chakra activation process. Although I was keen on my regular meditation practice, I did not have chakra activation as a desired goal. My work as a Human Resource Development Consultant for the Ministry of Local Government in Botswana, in charge of all training and testing activities for 6000 personnel, was complicated and heavy. As favoritism was rampant I was reluctant to delegate any of my important testing and grading work to others. Getting rid of the resultant mental stress was one of the reasons for my desire to meditate more regularly. Anyway achieving higher spiritual development in every possible way has been a major goal in my life and I have continued to receive abundant guidance and support of higher intelligences in these activities. Although I was aware that chakra activation was a major milestone in the spiritual development process, like the blossoming of a tree, I felt that it was best to let it grow at its own pace. Since I believe in reincarnation I was content to allow the chakra activation process to take place at its own speed, even if it had to take place in another life cycle. A number of books by Swami Vivekananda on different aspects of Yoga which I had obtained from the Ramakrishna Mission many years previously, but had not read completely, were lying with me and became my guide books on meditation at this time. We lived in a large house reserved for government executives, close to virgin jungle extending for hundreds of miles. These houses were surrounded by large gardens with myriad species of birds and animals, yet perfectly calm. I found this location to be ideally suited for my meditation. I meditated alone for about 45 minutes every night, whenever possible. It was a very simple kind of meditation. I did not follow any particular method or technique of meditation, but used my previous knowledge and practices of different religious systems wherever they seemed applicable. I had joined group meditations at Buddhist temples at different times, but was unable to obtain any lasting benefits. But this time I was more serious and determined to allow the natural progression of meditation without a pause. I sat alone in a room and closed the doors following Christ's advice on how to pray, as mentioned in the gospel of St. Mathew. At that time I did not find much difference between prayer and meditation. I used my Subud practice of testing whenever I felt the need for guidance. For example on one occasion when I had an uneasy feeling before starting to meditate, I resorted to Subud testing and came up with the idea that on such occasions I should quietly walk round my meditation mat and cushion several times before starting to meditate. It worked perfectly well. I started with self-remembering following the instructions I had received in Gurdjieff work and Buddhism. In the eightfold path of Buddhism, described in a previous chapter, meditation being the eighth and final step of the eight-fold path had to be immediately preceded by the seventh step of self-remembering, called samma sati, which means right attention and constant awareness of oneself.

I sat on a carpet, with the base of my spinal column resting on a firm cushion. I kept my legs crossed, right leg on the left, keeping the body perfectly erect. I have had some previous practice of trying to sit in the lotus pose, as depicted in statues of Lord Buddha. I spent a few minutes to relax my body and my mind, while maintaining self-remembering. As my thought process slowed down I could feel the meditation getting deeper and my mind starting to get enveloped in a pleasant stillness. Although there was a common pattern, each session of meditation was different. Sometimes I might hear distant sounds of music that I had not heard before or see glimmering lights of different colors and shapes, but I took care not to be carried away by such distractions. At this time we discovered several others in our community who were interested in group meditation. My wife came across a small meditation group at the house of an American lady who invited us to join their weekly group meditation. The group gradually expanded to contain those from other countries such as USA, Thailand and Burma who were interested in joining a meditation group. I joined the weekly group meditation while continuing with my daily solitary meditation, which I always preferred.

During this time I picked up a book on Zen training at a bookshop clearance sale. The name of the book was Zen Training by Katsuki Sekida. Later I discovered this to be a reputed classic on the subject. I found the book to be immensely useful. Finding this book was a meaningful synchronicity. It was an excellent guidebook on meditation but contained nothing about chakra activation. I meditated every night following the guidelines described in the book on Zen Training and the books by Vivekananda, as closely as possible. I followed more and more of Sekida's advice and found them useful. However I never followed any borrowed system for too long as I seemed to find it more useful to go with the flow of my own energies. I got into the habit of starting the meditation by a few deep breaths using the lower abdomen. Normally I meditated for at least 40 minutes, sometimes continuing for about an hour, and always felt deeply relaxed and energized. I was quite happy and contented as this satisfied my goals of meditation at that time.

I started my meditation sessions with awareness and self-remembering, paying attention to the sitting posture and breathing, without any attempt to skip the preliminaries. There is normally a tendency to go direct to deeper states of meditation. I learned from experience that it is not correct to rush through. I tried to slow down my thought process gradually by trying to observe and hold attention on the breathing. I tried to be relaxed and happy maintaining self-awareness. I learned to deal with thoughts as they came. Unless I remembered something that needed immediate attention, like leaving the bathroom water tap open, I let the thought slowly drift out of the field of attention. The main idea is not to allow it to form a chain of thoughts. In the earlier stages I kept a notebook and pencil close to me, but did not find it necessary later. I got into the habit of starting the meditation by slow and deep breathing using the lower abdomen, in a particular rhythm. After reading Sekida s book I made every fifth exhalation, longer and deeper than the others somewhat similar to what Sekida called the bamboo method of breathing. The usual pattern is 1. in-breath, 2. out-breath, 3. in-breath, 4. out-breath, 5. in-breath, 6. out-breath, 7. in-breath, 8. out-breath. 9. in-breath, 10. extra long out-breath emptying the lungs. Instead of counting it could be convenient to repeat a mantra or prayer with ten syllables to keep thoughts out. For example I used the first two sentences of the Lord s prayer arranged in ten steps this way. Our-father-which-art-in-heaven-hallowed-be-thy-name, with a deep exhalation at the last syllable while pronouncing "name". Sometimes I used the Buddhist chant "Namo-thassa-bhaga-vatho-ara-hatho-sam-ma-sambud-Dhassa". Many Hindus repeat the two syllables "so" and "ham" while breathing in and breathing out. Counting from one to ten may be the easiest for most of us. I keep on repeating this routine as long as comfortable or till I feel the activation of chakras, at which point I surrendered the controls to the kundalini energy.

After a few months of regular practice, I began feeling movements of energy inside my body during meditation. The first sign was a feeling of a spot of light or energy rotating in circles within my body. It occurred sporadically outside my control forming different sizes of circles and changing angles. I did not take much notice at the beginning. However when it started happening more frequently I took notice and started observing the patterns of movement. It took quite some time for me to recognize these movements within myself as the commencement of chakra or kundalini activity. At the beginning I ascribed them to the movements I used to feel in my Subud latihans which I have described elsewhere. I then realized that these energy manifestations were different from the Subud movements for a number of reasons. While Subud latihan movements were unpredictable and differed from session to session in unexpected ways, the energy manifestations in meditation had continuity; they were regular and involved only certain areas of the body. At this stage I started reading Vivekananda s Raja Yoga seriously and could see how his descriptions of chakra activation matched my experiences This way, my kundalini and chakra awakening process was quite gradual and fully spontaneous. It did not come with a sudden show of energy, rather it was a process of gradual growth from normal meditation, followed by the first signs of chakra movements, taking more than three months to complete the manifestation of all chakras. The process progressed naturally and it was totally joyful. On my part I did not push it or try to hasten it in any way. This may be the reason why I never had any negative manifestations, either physically or mentally.

After I continued my meditations in this fashion for a number of months, I started feeling that vibrational energy produced at each chakra was different, somewhat like the difference in the progressive notes of a musical octave. Vibrational energy produced by each chakra helped in the activation of the next higher chakra. It brought to my mind what I had learned in the theory and practice of music about sympathetic vibration, chords and principles of harmony. I could see the similarity of the seven chakra kundalini energy system to the seven notes of the musical octave. Further, I could see it matching with another similar octave like set of vibrational energies in the higher dimension of cosmic vibrations, where each of the seven holarchies generated vibrational energies forming what Gurdjieff described as octaves of cosmic energy, in which each holarchy level of cosmic entities produced progressively ascending energies, behaving like notes in a musical octave. This is sometimes called the music of the spheres. With time I started associating each activated chakra with a corresponding holarchic level linked through sympathetic vibration and reinforcing each other.

Let me describe my experience of what actually happens at a meditation session. when chakra activation commences. Normally it started at the location of the first chakra, which is at the base of the spinal column. It started with a gentle warmth accompanied by a subtle vibration sometimes like a very slight cramp in the area, indicating the commencement of a chakra activation. At this time I surrender myself to this energy in order to give it full freedom to manifest freely. This is accompanied by a spontaneous feeling of ecstasy. After a little while, the focus of the kundalini manifestation shifted to the second chakra in the genital area. I also sensed that the rate of vibration of the first chakra was in harmony with that of the first holarchy at the level of atoms. At each higher chakra the rate of vibration accelerated to that of the next level of holons in the cosmic holarchy. Thus at the second chakra I felt the energy of the cell with a harmonious connection to all other cells through the corresponding rate of vibration. When at the next stage the point of activation shifted to the solar plexus, which is the seat of the third chakra, the new rate of vibration was in harmony with that of living beings. The next chakra, which activated is the fourth, located in the chest area that stood for Gaia or planet earth. The rate of vibration of kundalini energy at this stage was in harmony with planet earth and all other planets, which now become the focus of attention. At the fifth chakra, at the neck level, the rate of vibration of Kundalini energy accelerates to be in harmony with the sun, which is the fifth level of holons in our holarchy. The next chakra, which is the sixth, at the level of the eyebrows, is in harmony with the rate of vibration of our galaxy, which is called the Milky Way. The dimension and rate of vibration of the galaxy is far higher than that of the sun represented by the fifth chakra. The final and the highest chakra in the human body is the seventh at the top of the head, representing the universe that consists of all the galaxies. The universe represents the three dimensional part of the multi-dimensional Cosmos. At this level, the meditator is in perfect harmony with the energy of the Universe. Even a few seconds at this high-energy dimension is capable of charging you up with immense energy of the highest type that could lead to development in all aspects of human life. Through principles of sympathetic vibration activated chakras link up with the celestial entities at parallel holarchies. Seen this way, a successful chakra meditation is equal to an excursion of the entire Universe covering all levels of holons from atoms to the Cosmos.

With time the chakra activation process got more stabilized and the sessions proceeded smoothly. Normally all seven chakras got progressively activated at each session of meditation. However although all chakras could get activated in a meditation session, the process is not at all automatic, as it requires continuous attention, self-awareness and concentration. Whenever attention failed and the mind was not properly centered the process faded off imperceptibly.

If I found it difficult to meditate on some days I accepted it without getting disturbed. I never allowed my meditation to skip personal or social obligations, which I accepted willingly. I would be satisfied if I could meditate four or five times a week.

There is no guarantee that commencement of chakra activation could be accurately predicted or hastened by routine preliminaries. The fact is that all human beings have them in a potential state, with a possibility of getting activated when the prerequisites are fulfilled. Prerequisites for meditation, in which chakra activation is manifested as an end product, are described in books on yoga. I prefer the older books which are simpler and more genuine. One of my favorites is Vivekananda s Raja Yoga. Most prerequisites deal with behavioral purity and mental clarity. All religions provide the guidelines for achieving these. The Ten Commandments of Christianity, and the eight-fold path of Buddhism are good examples. For those who believe in reincarnation there is no pressure to experience all spiritual manifestations within one's present life span, provided the process of preparation continues without interruption. I did not yearn for chakra activation and the fact that it manifested without much effort may be due to my cosmic consciousness experience facilitating the process. If one feels a constant desire for chakra activation, that may be a sign that the prerequisites are gradually being fulfilled. Patience would be needed. In meditation and chakra activation I could observe all my separately cultivated spiritual practices and knowledge working in parallel and in harmony, generating powerful synergies.

Gurdjieff taught that each of seven cosmic levels generate a different rate of vibrations which form an octave. As the human body is recognized as a microcosm of the cosmos, the seven chakras or energy centers correspond to the seven cosmic levels. Through the principle of sympathetic vibration each chakra corresponds to a cosmic level with which it forms a link. This made it possible for me to see the meaning of Gurdjieff's analogy of the musical octave to explain the increasing rates of vibration in each of the seven cosmic or holarchy levels. As each successive chakra generates an ascending note in parallel to the octave of cosmic vibrations, it is possible to surmise links of sympathetic vibration between corresponding chakras and holarchy levels. When I had a chakra activation I could feel this operation of sympathetic vibration links between chakras and cosmic holarchy dimensions.

A table showing the position of the seven chakras, their names and parallel holarchy levels is given below

> The First chakra Muladhara – at the base of the spinal column. Dormant kundalini energy is said to reside here as a coiled serpent. Kundalini means coiled in Sanskrit. (the level of energy and consciousness at this chakra corresponds to the first holarchy level which is that of the atom.)

The second chakra Swadhisthana – at the sex center. (The level of energy and consciousness is that of the cell).

The third chakra Manipura at the level of the solar plexus. (The level of energy and consciousness is that of human beings and other similar living beings)

The fourth chakra Anahata – chest level, (The level of energy and consciousness is that of Gaia/earth and planets)

The fifth chakra Vishudda – neck level,(the level of energy and consciousness is that of our sun and other suns)

The sixth chakra Ajna – forehead level. (The level of energy and consciousness is that of our galaxy, milky way and other galaxies.)

The seventh chakra Sahasrara – top of the head, meaning the lotus of the hundred thousand petals.(The level of energy and consciousness is that of our Universe and other universes.)

In the course of a chakra meditation the expansion of one's field of energy and consciousness from the level of the atom at the first chakra, to the level of the cell at the second chakra, to the level of living beings at the third center, to the level of gaia as planet earth at the fourth chakra, to the level of sun at the fifth center, to the level of the galaxy at the sixth center and to the level of the universe or cosmos at the seventh center is a profound experience. It needs the continuation of one's total concentration with prayer, self-remembering and meditation. This to me is the highest benefit of chakra meditation, which enables the sharing of energies at each level of the holarchy, with resultant benefits in the areas of health and vitality, mental and emotional development and spiritual growth.

Chakras are multifunctional energy centers. Each of the seven chakras has to be understood as a self-contained energy center serving a number of functions. They are units of energy production, energy accumulation or storage, and energy distribution. They also act as energy transformers and energy transducers. Through principles of sympathetic vibration chakras find harmonies and establish links with corresponding cosmic dimensions or holarchy levels. Such linkages are beneficial as they enable sharing and exchange of energies with higher entities at cosmic or holarchy levels. As harmonic linking of centers through sympathetic vibration enables the sharing of energy with higher entities at all holarchic levels each energy center represents a particular level in the vast network of the cosmic energy system as shown in the table.

Through a combination of the chakra ladder with the holarchy progression new possibilities and avenues open up for experiencing the ascending and progressively expanding levels of holarchy through inner kundalini energy centers and paths. I felt spontaneously that each level of chakra activation brought awareness and harmony with each of the ascending levels of holons in the holarchy. I also found meaning in Gurdjieff's analogy of the musical octave in which the activation of each successive chakra generates an ascending note in the octave of cosmic vibrations. This gives a new significance to chakra activation as a means of producing higher cosmic energies.

Chapter 16

Near Death Experience

What I am giving here is a detailed account of my own Near-death experience. Although it may sound paradoxical and hard to believe, I can confess with sincerity that my NDE is one of the best experiences of my life. Even a passing memory of it fills my entire body mind system with inexpressible love and joy. I have no doubt that it was a continuation and complement to my childhood cosmic consciousness experience, giving me still more insights of spirituality and adding meaning to my later life and the inevitable process of death. I learned many new lessons in my NDE, removing all fear of death from my mind, and revealing the unlimited presence of love in the higher realms of spirituality and the unlimited potential of love both in human life and all cosmic levels of life. It prompted me to share my love with all beings without any reservations or limitations.

During the latter part of 1993, I felt a slight heaviness in the chest area when I got up in the mornings. Occasionally I had to recline myself using several pillows to make my breathing easier. When I mentioned this to my doctor, he advised me to get my heart examined by a cardiologist and arranged for several tests including a stress test in which I had to use an inclined walker with heart monitoring devices attached to my chest area. After examining the test results, he advised me to get an angiogram to determine whether the heart arteries are affected. A dye was injected to my vascular system to see the working of the arteries more clearly. I could see an inverted picture of my heart on a TV monitor, which displayed the arteries clearly. He pointed to me several areas of the heart arterial system, which he said were blocked by plaque. Frankly, I could not see anything clearly but had to depend on what he was saying. The cardiologist determined that I would need heart bypass surgery for which he had to refer me to a heart surgeon. At an interview with a heart surgeon he tried to explain to me the urgent need for heart bypass surgery and fixed an early date for the operation. The bypass surgery was fixed for 10/01/93 at the West Hills Regional Medical Center in Southern California. On the day of the operation, while I was being wheeled into the operating theater, my mind was absolutely calm as I surrendered myself to God. I had no anxiety about thoughts of death. I came out of the anesthesia in good condition and remember eating a cup of jelly while seated on the bed. After about 24 hours, my condition deteriorated due to a piece of plaque blocking a principle artery in the apex region of the heart causing a heart attack, described as a myocardial infarction. The hospital authorities woke up my wife at 3 o clock in the morning with the news that my condition had deteriorated and was critical and that they had to start using a balloon device to assist in my breathing. At this stage, I had lost consciousness, or rather; I had passed on to a different dimension of consciousness. I felt the presence of a crowd of dwarf-like beings surrounding me and announcing to me that I am dying. I was not in the least disappointed and surrendered myself to whatever is to come. Next I found myself floating through a dark space with a light at the further end, which I recognized to be my destination. My mind was quite tranquil. While floating forward toward the light I noticed a much fainter light on my left side. I seemed to have the option of continuing to move forward or diverting to the left toward the smaller light, which seemed to beckon me. I then started moving toward the smaller light, which emanated from an octagonal tower of an ancient building that appeared to be similar to the tooth-relic temple in the city of Kandy in Sri Lanka. Kneeling before a votary oil-lamp was my wife. I knew at once that she was praying for my life. As I approached closer she looked at me with tearful eyes of most tender love and moved up to join me spontaneously. We then started floating through space together, side by side, as if we were journeying through space together, in an invisible vehicle. In trying to recollect the mode of travel I feel that our bodies were side by side, stretched flat face downwards, similar to the scenes of astral traveling in the movie "What dreams may come." Our path of travel was incredibly beautiful as we passed through colorful twilight scenes. In some areas there was a resemblance to Sri Lankan hill country tea gardens as were familiar to us when we lived in the Badulla tea plantation areas.

I became aware of a temporary change of scene. I was now lying down on a magnificent bed of utmost comfort with plush bed linen, in a majestic setting with carved heavy-wood furniture. Soft music mixed with unusually comforting vibrations of melodious chanting are heard in the background. Tall erect women in long classical-like attire carrying sweet smelling incense bowls were walking up and down so gently as if floating in the air. I felt myself being healed by a soothing energy. I felt the presence of an entity with immense healing powers directing attention on me, although I was unable to see any one directly. I felt the soothing activation of a powerful healing energy as I rested peacefully. I felt very inquisitive to find out what this place is where I am being healed, and by what entity. I seemed to receive an answer that this was a sacred temple of Tibetan Buddhism. I pledged to myself that when I am fully healed I would express my gratitude by devoting time and energy to explore this path and practice its tenets.

I wondered what role the surgeon, my doctor and the medical team who are supposed to heal me through surgery are playing. As if in reply to my thought I see them busy, doing nothing important in a basement. The next scene is that of my return. As I saw myself returning to my bed I felt incredibly sad and frustrated. If not for the love of my dear wife and the children I would have opted to get back to that dimension where I was enjoying bliss without any pain or sorrow.

While I was going through these NDE adventures, my wife who was lucky enough to have our son visit her by sheer synchronicity, were having stressful experiences with my doctors and hospital staff. On the day of my heart attack and blackout, my wife received a telephone call from the hospital that my condition was hopeless. She immediately fell on her knees in prayer, and had a vision of Sathya Sai Baba in a blue form. This comforted her, particularly as she knew that blue is the color of healing. This may have been the time when I met her during my NDE, in a moment of prayer. There was nothing more they could do till on the third day I could open my eyes, to everybody's surprise and tried to communicate with them with great difficulty.

To me my Near Death Experience was a deep spiritual revelation with no connection to any particular religion. It was an experience of unconditional love and compassion pervading all life. I felt from deep within me that God cares only about love and inner spirituality without any concern for religious affiliation. It was a demonstration that the way to heaven is through pure love, which is not related to any religion because religion is a social institution while love and spirituality are universal and divine.

My healing was a gradual process as my physical energy was very low. I had to undergo many types of tests and therapy. My speech and communication, which was at a very low level, improved gradually. Some time after the incident, I made attempts to visit any Tibetan temples in California, but none of them were successful. My wife joined me in visiting a few temples and attending seminars of visiting Tibetan Lamas. They were sometimes expensive, but did not serve our purpose. It was in 2003, that we found what we were searching for. We had to change our physician. One of my close friends mentioned that his physician is a Tibetan doctor, whom he strongly recommended. I thought this might help me to find admission to a Tibetan temple, and applied to have him as my physician. I succeeded in getting myself registered under the Tibetan doctor as my family physician, and also to find admission to a weekly Tibetan ceremony. At the first Tibetan religious ceremony I attended, I could hear the very same type of chanting heard by me in my Near Death Experience. I had no doubt that I had found the right place. People who all through their lives had very strong feelings of antagonism towards religions other than their own have reported that after their NDEs these feelings changed to feelings of love to all religions without any trace of previous antagonism. Another significant advantage is that in an NDE one is given the opportunity to learn and grow spiritually and get prepared for the next life without any fear of death.

Chapter 17

Experience in Kataragama vortexes

KATARAGAMA is an area in the southern part of Sri Lanka, where surrounded by thick jungle on all sides there is an ancient shrine dating back to pre-christian times. The shrine and the surrounding area are charged by a strong spiritual presence. Since I have had several experiences of unmistakable spiritual power in this area where a Hindu shrine and a Buddhist dagoba are situated side by side, I decided to include a description of it in this book. I tend to believe that this site could have had a spiritual significance even before these shrines were built.

From ancient times it was common for people from different parts of the country to visit Kataragama through jungle routes infested with wild animals. Now the road system is developed providing easy access to the area including the shrine. While I was working for the Sri Lanka government as an Assistant Commissioner of Local Government, I was fortunate to have this area within my area of authority as it enabled me to visit the place as often as I liked on government duty. This area had a special appeal to me as I have had several remarkable spiritual experiences at this place. It is situated in a small township in the deep south of Sri Lanka about 180 miles south of Colombo, the capital of Sri Lanka. According to the great chronicle of Sri Lankan history called Mahawamsa, when the Bo-sapling (a branch of the Bodhi tree under which Gotama Buddha attained enlightenment in Buddha Gaya in North India 2500 years ago) was brought to Anuradhapura from India 2300 years ago, the warriors (Kshatriyas) from Katharagama were present on the occasion to pay homage and respect. It is also recorded in historical epics that Lord Buddha, in his third and the last visit to Sri Lanka met King Mahasena who ruled over the Kataragama area in B.C.580. The Kirivehera Dagoba which stands in close proximity to the Devale was built by the King Mahasena. Thus Sri Lankans believe that Kataragama was sanctified by Lord Buddha. Katharagama God is indigenous and long-celebrated in Sri Lankan lore and legend, and originally resides on the top of mountain called Waedahiti Kanda just outside of the Katharagama town. Since ancient times an inseparable connection between the God and his domain has existed. The God Kataragama's image is depicted either with six heads and 12 hands, or one head and 4 hands. The God's vehicle is the peacock, which is native to Sri Lanka and India. Multiple heads denote omniscience while multiple arms denote omnipotence. Irrespective of caste and creed, all Sri Lankans show great reverence to God Kataragama. They honor him as a very powerful deity and beg divine help to overcome their personal problems or for success in business enterprises, etc, with the fervent hope that their requests would be granted. They believe that God Kataragama actually exists and is vested with extraordinary power to assist those who appeal to him with faith and devotion in times of their distress or calamity. Kataragama is a multi-religious sacred city as it contains an Islamic Mosque within its Devale complex as well. It holds its annual festival, that celebrates the God's courtship and marriage to a Vedda princess, in July to August. These references in historical documents provide authentic evidence that the shrine at Kataragama has a history dating back to pre-Christian times.

On one of my official visits to Kataragama I was disturbed to see devotees undergoing great physical suffering as they pulled vehicles which were attached to their bodies by metal hooks. Such acts of penance are performed by those who pledge such suffering in return for favors received from the god such as being healed of an incurable disease. Very often there are hundreds of devotees doing penance of different descriptions. A popular penance done as a reward for a very high divine favor is participation in the annual fire walking ceremony. That day I was particularly disturbed about the suffering of devotees and wondered about the nature of power being manifested in this shrine. That afternoon after my lunch I was seated in a comfortable lounge chair at the government rest house. I was resting with my eyes closed although still quite awake, when I suddenly saw some brightly illuminated letters as seen in in neonsigns. The letters were in Sinhala. The meaning of the six-word phrase is "Thousands of manifestations, but one destination" (Dahas gane balatala eti ekama iranama.) I could not understand what it meant quite clearly, and immediately noted it down in my notebook. After a few minutes, as I closed my eyes again, I saw an illuminated phrase in English, which read "WILL OF THE WORLD". I noted it too and started thinking about their meanings. It did not take me long to realize that they were direct answers to my negative thoughts and doubts about the shrine a few hours earlier. That

evening I visited a highly educated swami who was
known to me and lived in a small hut close to the
shrine. I have had interesting discussions with swami
Shanmuga Vadivel earlier. He was highly educated
and I have had many discussions about spiritual
matters with him. He was delighted to hear about my
experience and gave me many references to ancient
scriptures and modern metaphysical writings, which
clarified very lucidly the hidden meaning of the
phrases that were revealed to me. He explained that
the word "will" referred to the presence of life and
the phrase "WILL OF THE WORLD" meant that
planet earth is the living entity, which is in control of
this shrine and the surrounding area. This explains
how thousands of miracles take place here, and why
devotees from different parts of Sri Lanka, and even
from India visit this place repeatedly. We discussed
the concept of high-energy spots on Earth that are
generally called vortices. Vortices appear to be points
of power or energy on the Earth, while ley lines
are the links between those points. Vortices are the
parallels of chakras in the human body. Recently I
visited Sedona in Arizona and as I felt the power of
the vortices my thoughts went back to Kataragama
where I had experienced similar energies. The
Internet has several web sites describing the ley lines
and vortices. For example, http://www.lifeoflight.
com/PowerSites/power-indme.html#indme

Thus my vision of meaningful words of divine origin as mentioned above removed all doubts and negative thoughts that I had in my mind about this holy place and shrine. I was fully convinced that this is indeed a holy spot, where through a natural concentration of spiritual energy, divine omnipotence and omniscience dispense divine grace for devotees, similar to other holy sites in different parts of the earth. i.e. in Hawaii, The Bahamas, the Red Sea, Australia.

There is plenty of ongoing research about high-energy spots on earth, and their relationship to spiritual development and awareness. Such vortices are found to enhance spiritual sensitivity and therefore provide ideal spots for activities such as meditation and traditional ceremonies for attuning with earth's energies. Indian Americans have used spots such as Sedona for their spiritual activities from ancient times. Kataragama can provide unmistakable evidence for such investigations. It is one of the very few locations where an annual fire-walking ceremony is open for public viewing. The swami told me that the manifestations that appeared to be strange to my mind were quite suited and acceptable to the belief patterns of devotees in that sacred environment, and that it is wrong for me to consider such manifestations as negative.

Chapter 18

Other Remarkable Experiences in My Life

Some Case Studies in Synchronicity

There have been many unusual incidents in my life, which show evidence of being guided and protected by higher powers. The word used for such meaningful coincidences is synchronicity. Analyzing personal experiences involving synchronicity is the best means of increasing one's knowledge and sensitivity of how spiritual manifestations can be recognized in real life. Some incidents in my life suitable for such analysis are described in this section. The samples described below could give the reader an understanding of their nature. In my opinion they provide evidence of the process of synchronicity, which when acknowledged with thankfulness and positive intentions may pave the way for more of such occurrences in keeping with one's intentions.

a. Tow Truck without ordering

The first incident is about my car skidding into a muddy paddy field in Gampaha. At that time, I had a driver because I had to travel alone to remote areas in hilly regions where the roads were narrow, irregular and meandering. One day, I was returning to my home in Kalutara for a weekend from my hill station in Matale. It was around midnight when a very heavy thunderstorm started. My driver was driving too fast despite my warnings. Suddenly, the car started skidding and the driver was unable to control the car, which skidded and went off the road and fell into a rice field, which was about 8 feet below the road. Because of the rain the rice field had got very muddy and about half of the car was embedded in the mud. It was with great difficulty that I opened the door and managed to wade through the mud and climb on all fours to the road. My body and clothes were fully covered with mud. I was surprised to see a car stopped and waiting for us. The driver of the car, a neatly dressed gentleman said that he was following my car when at that point he suddenly lost sight of my car in the thunderstorm and knew that there was a problem. Therefore he stopped his car and was waiting to inform somebody so that they could start looking for my car. Although it was close to midnight and heavily raining some people gathered and took stock of the situation. They mentioned that at least twenty people would be needed to pull the car out, but it is unlikely to get so many people at that hour. The other alternative was to get a tow-truck from Colombo, which could take three to four days, apart from the high cost. While we were discussing the hopelessness of the situation, a heavy vehicle appeared on the road and stopped on seeing the crowd. The driver of the vehicle mentioned that their vehicle was a new and sophisticated type of tow truck used for large government construction projects. They could easily pull out the mud buried car. They had all the equipment such as chains and pulleys and within 15 minutes they could pull the car out onto the road, and they went their way without any mention of a payment. Everybody was so surprised about my good luck in being able to get the car onto the road. To me it was an example of synchronicity, which is difficult to understand except as a case of divine intervention. It was God's grace that a heavy tow truck, which was very rarely seen on those roads passed through just at that time.

b. The book I wanted found in the trash

I have had unusual luck with finding books required by me. I was writing my doctoral thesis for the University of Metaphysics when I had to honor a deadline. I needed a copy of "Varieties of Religious Experience" by James for some references. I went to the closest Metaphysical bookshop where I thought I could find it, either new or used. I was very frustrated not to be able to get it there. While leaving the bookshop I saw a heap of very old books waiting to be disposed or trashed. I looked at it casually, and right on the top of the heap of books was a copy of the book I was searching for. I was asked to pick it up free. I prayed thanking God for the favor. I have had immense luck at bookshops. Several times a book falls at my feet matching my need exactly.

c. Spiritual GPS (Global Positioning System)

Joining Subud and practicing latihans awakens in oneself a remarkable ability to test what is right and wrong. On several occasions at that time I proceeded to test this power and have had incredible results. After getting married at Matara I received a transfer to another region in the country, called Badulla. I had never traveled to this area,

WHY I LIVE | 163

but had maps which could be used to reach our destination. At the beginning of the trip I decided to be guided mainly by testing in the subud style and not to use maps unless we really get lost

The first part was easy as there were large sign boards guiding motorists to different towns. But the task got more complicated after entering the city area. When I came to a junction I had to determine whether to go straight, turn left or turn right. By using my subud testing technique I had to find our way. After passing many junctions and traveling several miles we reached an area, which seemed to match the description of the terrain as had been described to us. We thought it best to inquire and found that we have come within sight of our destination, which was the home of Sreeni's friends, with whom we were going to live till we find a house for ourselves. The rest was easy. Our faith in Subud testing was confirmed beyond any doubt.

d. Surgery Avoided

During our early years in Badulla I had severe pains in my abdomen and was diagnosed with Appendicitis and was recommended surgery. Because Badulla was a regional town medical facilities were poor. We found that the hospital was not well staffed and that there was only one'surgeon. Further there was a long waiting line, for a surgery. However I registered myself for the surgery and surrendered myself to God. I also wrote a letter to Bapak, founder of the Subud movement (in Indonesia) mentioning about my having to undergo surgery, and requesting for his blessings and prayers. In three weeks I received an airmail letter from Indonesia with a message from Bapak's secretary. It said that Bapak has prayed for me and feels that I do not need surgery. We found it necessary to take a major decision of life and death based on faith. The decision was made easy by the fact that I did not suffer any pain since the receipt of the letter. Thanks to God and Bapak I was fully recovered with no recurrence of the pain ever after. This was a major miracle in my life.

e. Car stops by itself to save the life of a child

My work in Badulla involved plenty of driving on narrow roads with houses on both sides of the road. One day I was returning after a long trip. I was passing a large truck, which had been stopped on the side of the road. The road was clear of traffic and I was driving fairly fast at about 40 miles per hour. While passing the truck I spontaneously applied my brakes quite suddenly without any reason. The car came to a screeching halt in level with the front of the stationcry truck. To my utter amazement, a young girl of about four years ran across the road, within three feet of the front of the car followed by her mother. It was impossible for me to see the child because of the truck. I would not have been able to save her if not for my being made to stop the car by an outside power. Everybody present thanked me for being smart enough to save the child. I stopped the car by the side of the road and prayed before proceeding.

f. Saved from a Poisonous Snake

During the latter part of our nine years in Badulla we lived in a beautiful government owned house at the top of a hill. There were two rooms on either side of the large sitting room in the center. Our bedrooms were on the right side. One day I slept in one of the left side visitor's rooms because I had influenza, from which I wanted to protect my wife and child. I read in bed and had fallen asleep with the light still on. Around midnight I was awakened by a very loud cry from my infant child. As I did not hear my wife waking up, I got up to walk across to their bedroom. As the light was still on, I could see a large snake crawling towards my bed. I was quite scared, as I knew that there were plenty of poisonous snakes in this area. I stood up on the bed watching the snake and called my wife asking her to inform our neighbors. The snake stopped moving and I dared to rush out of the room. Our neighbors came in and killed the snake. It was easy because the lights were on. Our neighbors knew about snakes and identified the snake to be a very poisonous species. The most significant part of the story is that my wife assured me that our child never cried. I was made to hear that cry of a child as a means of saving me from the poisonous snake that was heading towards my bed.

g. Risorgimento

Badulla where I was officially posted as Asst Commissioner of Local Government was about 6 hours driving distance from my home in Wellawatte where my father and mother lived. Although I made an effort to visit them at least once in two months, pressure of work did not allow me to come that often. I loved my mother dearly. Whenever I visited her, she was overjoyed. On one of my visits I found her suffering from a bad attack of asthma. I was very sad to leave her while she was in that condition. A few days before I was to leave, a strange word came to my mind at night but I was unable to recollect it the following morning. All my efforts to recollect the strange word were in vain. The word recurred the following night too. For fear of losing it again, I scribbled it on the wall closest to me with a pencil. The strange word was risorgimento, a word I had never heard before. I went through all the dictionaries in the house but was unable to find it. I took it down in my notebook as I had to leave the following day. When I reached my work station at Badulla I made another vain effort to find the meaning of the word. As I had to leave for outstation work in different distant locations, I lost track of my desire to search for its meaning. A few weeks later I received a message that my mother had expired due to a medical mishap. I was very surprised to learn this sad news and made arrangements to leave for Colombo as soon as possible. My brother telephoned asking me to pick up a wreath and some flowers he had ordered from a florist shop, which was on my way. I immediately asked him to place an additional order for a wreath on behalf of our family and promised to pick up the wreath and flowers as requested. When I dropped in at the florist they wanted me to come 15 minutes later as they were still working on the second wreath. Adjoining the florist shop there was a large bookshop which I had visited a number of times. To while away the time I entered the bookshop and picked up a book from the first shelf I passed, even without looking at the name of the book. I opened the book at random and to my great surprise saw the word risorgimento on that page. I was shocked at this coincidence; I should call it synchronicity. The book I had picked up, even without looking at the cover, was a Pelican Dictionary of History and the article in which this word occurred was titled "The Unification of Italy". The word risorgimento means resurrection in Italian, and was used as the name of the movement for the unification of Italy. Why was the word revealed to me on my last visit to my mother? I immediately saw the message this word was meant to convey to me. My mother's death was not accidental. It was her time for death and resurrection. This synchronicity game me immense solace.

h. Using a Citreon Club Car saved our lives.

My first United Nations consultancy was at the African Center for Administration and Research based in Morocco. We lived there for over three years. I bought a Citroen Club car from my colleague who held that position previously. A few months after we settled down we received an invitation for an evening party from one of my new friends. Because we were expecting to meet many new people, we dressed up neatly and Sreeni wore some of her expensive gold jewelry. We carried a paper with the directions to the house, but being new to the city of Tangier we lost the way. We stopped the car at a wayside retail outlet where some people were seen outside, to ask for directions. One of the men mentioned that his home is in that area and volunteered to show us the way if we could give him a ride. We agreed and asked him to sit in the rear seat. After a few miles he asked us to turn to a side road. When I questioned why it was necessary, he said that the side road was a shortcut to the road where our friend's house was. After some distance the side road became narrower and rocky. I felt that he had murderous intentions in his mind and planned a way of escaping. I told him that I had to get down from the car and see if I can take it over the rocks on the road. He mentioned that we do not have to go far and he too got down from the car. Then I smelt that he has taken drugs and felt that we are now at his mercy and that he could be eyeing Sreeni's jewelry. I clearly felt that we had to escape from him in any possible way. I did not show my fear but prayed for a way of escape and asked him to walk in front of the car till we passed the rocks. He agreed and walked past the car. As soon as he was at a safe distance, I engaged the special gear that is a feature of Citroen Club cars to increase the clearance, and reversed a short distance as fast as I could and made a U-turn taking care not to hit the rocks. Sreeni looked back and had seen the man chasing the car with a large rock in his hand. I drove at full speed to the main road and took the car to a spot where there was a light and a building. My silencer and attachments were missing but I could drive the car home. When I phoned my host and explained the incident he was so happy that we escaped from a drug addicted criminal and warned us never again to give rides to unknown people. We were saved from death by the grace of God and my sensitivity to God's message asking me to take prompt action to save ourselves. We would not have been able to escape if we were driving a car without the special Citroen gear, which made it possible to drive over the rocks.

Car expressing feelings

While working in Botswana we bought a new Toyota Cressida Car. I used it for my official work which sometimes involved traveling long distances in very remote areas, where roads were not paved or tarred and were in very bad condition. I never had any problems with my Cressida and I developed a special relationship with my car. When we had to leave Botswana for USA I felt sorry to part with the car. I decided to sell it to my best friend Gamini to whom I gave it at a very low price. He allowed me to use it till the last week of my stay in Botswana, and gave his car to be used during the last week. On the morning of my departure I had to go to Gamini's home to sign the car transfer papers. I parked Gamini's car near the gate and was trying to ring the door-bell when I saw my Cressida parked in his carport. I felt a pang of sorrow as it was my last glimpse of it. Suddenly the burglar alarm siren of the car started sounding and Gamini opened the door and was surprised to see me. When I explained what happened Gamini was very interested as he was a student of metaphysics. He told me that it was his best experience of telekinesis. Before I left I kissed the car good-bye. I have had many similar experiences showing that machines are alive and intelligent.

PART FOUR

SYNTHESIS

IV A

Introduction to Part IV

The sum total of one's concepts about himself and everything outside himself constitutes one's worldview. The limited worldview of my childhood centering round my home, family and neighborhood, progressively expanded through my education, varied spiritual development practices, ventures and experiences in many religious and metaphysical fields. In the first part of the book I described the activities of my childhood and youth, including a spontaneous cosmic consciousness experience, which looms large as the high point of my spiritual experience. This experience is described in detail in Chapter 14. I felt that the energies I contacted and merged with during that experience installed within me a strong spiritual center of gravity which gave me holistic guidance throughout the eventful journey of my life.

Christianity and Buddhism were the first disciplines I inherited from my parents during childhood. I learned of the concept of God and the validity of prayer from Christianity; Buddhism opened for me the doors of meditation, while Hinduism taught me the identity of self and the cosmos as Atman and Brahman. This spiritual foundation that stabilized within me in my early years helped me to recognize and join two spiritual paths that were correct for me at that time of spiritual growth. They were Gurdjieff work in my early twenties (see ch.10) and Subud (Susila Buddhi Dharma) in my early thirties (Ch11). They helped me immensely at that stage of development, particularly by giving me an inner ability to discern what is right and wrong for me. Susila Budhi Dharma (Subud) initiated me into a powerful energy and taught me a way of testing which could be used to find guidance whenever I needed to choose between alternative paths that lay open to me. It was like a personal oracle, which I could use freely in my decision-making. I have described my experiences with these spiritual paths in the second part of the book. In Part three of the book, I have disclosed for the first time a number of intimate and personal spiritual experiences, which provided valid proof of synchronicity and spiritual guidance and support I have continuously received in the past, and continue to receive in the present Part four that follows is a synthesis of my belief system using knowledge gathered through varied religious and metaphysical sources, modern scientific research, and my own creative thinking and inspiration.

Chapter 19

My Worldview

A World View is a mental framework that ties all our concepts and beliefs together to enable us to understand our place in the society, nation and the universe. It is always better to get a picture of the whole in the first place, rather than focusing on small patches of reality. A large work of art is best appreciated at the outset by viewing it from a sufficient distance to see it as a whole. One's Worldview is therefore a complex synthesis of one's past experiences and present belief systems, together with the knowledge of scientific discoveries, philosophical insights, and religious and metaphysical revelations. It is only with the background of such a holistic worldview that we could proceed to make realistic scenarios for the future.

One's worldview starts to take shape around one's concept of how it all started. How did everything originate? Was there a creation, a process of evolution or any other incomprehensible beginning? Creation is the biggest enigma of life. Scientists are exploring everywhere in the universe, from the smallest quarks to the largest quasars for clues to the origin of life. Although recent space probes are being watched with much excitement for any evidence of life in outer space, so far they have failed to come up with any significant clues. Theories relating to the creation of the Universe, such as Black Holes, the Big Bang and the Expansion of the Universe are isolated observations with nothing to bind them together into a plausible proposition.

Therefore it is best to start at the very beginning, by trying to understand how everything came into existence. While being aware that there are thousands of creation stories in different parts of the world, it is sufficient for our purposes to confine our thinking to the current theories of creation and evolution and relevant scientific concepts that are taken for granted by modern western society. I have to explain some elements of my belief system at the outset. Due to various activities and experiences during the course of my life as explained in the previous sections of this book, I have cultivated a deep faith in a supreme intelligence, which may be called by different names such as God, Dharma, Allah etc according to the religion into which one is born. My life experiences have crystallized in me an unshakeable belief in this supreme divine being for which I use the word God for convenience.

When Moses asked God for His name He replied, "I Am What I Am" to indicate that God did not have a personal name. The entity I call God was there from the beginning and will last forever. In my opinion He has no physical body as He has no need for any physical activities. As He is omnipotent and could get anything done, He has no need for arms or muscles. As God is already omniscient, He does not need a brain to think, or a head to protect the brain. As He is omnipresent He does not need legs, or vehicles to get about. In short God has no need for a body, and does not have one. When dealing with human beings He might take a human form to simplify the process of communication. I am aware that there is a problem in using the masculine third person singular in writing about God as He is neither male nor female. When I use the word He to mean God, it is devoid of a masculine connotation.

Those who formulated the attributes of God as omnipotent, omniscient and omnipresent seem to have lost sight of His all-pervading love, which to me is the most important. This makes it necessary to add a fourth attribute as omni-loving or all loving. Therefore we could say that God is omnipotent, omniscient, omnipresent, and also omni-loving.

It is impossible for me to believe that mere chance, without the participation of a higher intelligence such as an omniscient and omnipotent God, created the universe. God's artistic talent is an essential element of His omniscience. God's creativity includes the qualities of a master artist. An artist needs to manifest one's artistry by creating works of art. It would be natural for God the Almighty to desire to create a three-dimensional version of His multi-dimensional domain, just as a creative painter reduces the image of a picturesque three-dimensional landscape onto a two-dimensional canvas. I have devoted long hours to examine and recognize the validity of this concept, which to me provides a valuable clue to solve the enigma of how our three-dimensional universe came into being. I see our three dimensional universe as a work of art created by God as a reproduction of His multidimensional cosmos.

When Hubble discovered with his telescope the universally accepted phenomenon of the expanding universe, some scientists tried using the evidence to calculate the age of the universe. That appeared to them as a bright idea. They inferred that if the radiating lines of expansion are reversed in a computer model till they converge, they could thereby calculate the age of the universe. Through this means, they succeeded in calculating the age of the universe at approximately 15 billion years. Scientists considered it to be a great achievement. However they could not find any physical cause for the triggering off of such a massive process of expansion. For lack of any logical reason with valid evidence they called the beginning point the "Big Bang" assuming that a physical explosion caused the process of expansion of the universe. This appeared plausible to scientists who were confined to three-dimensional thinking.

I can see a number of reasons why the Big Bang theory could not be valid.

1. A random explosion cannot cause the beginning of a systematically organized and organic universe.
2. Before the universe came into being there was a complete void. In such a void there was no possibility of any explosion in the nature of the big bang. This raises a chicken or the egg type of dilemma, as to which came first, the big bang or the creation of the universe.
3. There could be reasons other than a physical explosion for setting into motion an expansion

of a large body such as the universe, as will be further discussed below.

In the rest of the chapter we will be examining possibilities for other ways in which an expansion of the universe could have originated. We have to keep in mind that scientists who are trapped in three-dimensional mind-sets are not likely to be able to comprehend multi-dimensional realities. Their being limited to only three-dimensional realities in their thinking and experimentation handicaps them. Their incapability to use their imagination freely beyond the limits imposed by their three-dimensional tools and mind-sets make them blind to realities outside the three-dimensional entities thereby limiting their range of vision. This explains the reluctance of scientists to see eye to eye with metaphysical or spiritual thinkers in spite of the fact that metaphysical sciences and religions have provided ample evidence of realities far beyond the three dimensional arena of scientific thinking.

What I give below is based on my thinking supported by the revelations I have had on the nature of the Cosmos in my cosmic consciousness experience, which was later collaborated and augmented by my own chakra experiences and a Near Death Experience. In my opinion, in any studies of the universe or cosmology involving a search for meaning or purpose, scientists need to collaborate with their colleagues in the areas of religious and metaphysical sciences.

The orderly arrangement of planetary bodies and the precision of their movements as demonstrated in astrology leave no doubt to their being the creation of an extremely high intelligence. It is impossible for a random explosion such as the imaginary Big-Bang to give rise to such an orderly universe which includes human beings like us with consciousness and high intelligence. The universe as we know it, has all the signs of being created by a super intelligence, which could be no other than the entity we call God. In the light of my revelations about the nature of the cosmos, in all my personal spiritual experiences, I feel inspired to present an alternative scenario. I appeal to all readers to use utmost patience in trying to understand my version. I respect the views of all those who have tried to understand the mystery of the origin of the cosmos. It is necessary to understand that God is an omni dimensional entity, which means that He could manifest himself or create new entities of any dimension. Our physical universe is only three-dimensional although the cosmos of which it is a part is multidimensional as it includes higher dimensions that are non-physical. Before the creation of our three dimensional universe, the three dimensional plane was void and empty. The creative mind of God, omnipotent and omniscient, visualized a new universe of three dimensions, with time as the fourth dimension. Before creating the universe, God formed within Himself a clear conceptual image of the detailed make up of the future universe He desired to create.

Some of the features of the plan He formulated for the Universe could be as follows: The entire Universe including all entities that form parts of the Universe, from the largest quasars to the smallest quarks was to consist of independent but inter-related living entities. Four energies, earth, water, air and fire, would serve as the forces activating the building blocks of the new Universe. All living entities within the universe were to form an inter-related organic structure in which smaller entities are parts of large entities, while large entities become parts of still larger entities, continuing this pattern of relationship from the smallest to the largest entities. In metaphysical terminology holon means a part of a whole. Every whole is at the same time a holon, as it is a part of a still larger whole. This pattern of relationship continues throughout to cover all entities from the smallest quark or atom to the largest galaxy or quasar. This hierarchical pattern of relationship of holons is called a holarchy. Although a universe may have an innumerable number of holarchical levels, our universe was planned to possess seven broad hierarchical levels as follows, with the universe itself as the highest or seventh. The seven broad levels are

Seventh – The Universe, three dimensional
            part of the cosmos
Sixth – Galaxies
Fifth – Suns
Fourth – Planets
Third – Living beings (human and
           sub-human)
Second – Cells
First – Atoms and particles.

He visualized the universe as a part of Himself, growing down from Himself progressively, as a holarchy of seven levels of holons. All holons, as living entities would be equipped with anatomical and physiological tools for activating the three basic modes of energy and life creation (anabolism), energy storage and balance (homeostasis) and energy utilization (katabolism). These three functions are described in the Hindu Trinity as Brahma, Vishnu and Shiva.

The higher living beings such as humans would have seven functional systems, namely circulatory system, digestive system, muscular system, nervous system, respiratory system, skeletal system and urinary/sexual system. All entities from the smallest to the largest would form an integrated holarchy, while maintaining communication with each other at all times. The entire system would be holographically integrated with each unit possessing all features of the whole. The entire Universe will go through processes of evolution enabling lower level entities to evolve from lower to higher forms of life. After God finished formulating His Plan for a grand cosmos, which included the creation of human beings in His own image at a later period, the stage was ready to activate His Master Plan for the Cosmo-genesis.

God caused the simultaneous creation of a male gamete and a female gamete, out of His yin and yang energies, for the production of the baby universe as His offspring. The two gametes united spontaneously to bring forth a one-cell zygote to serve as the parent cell of the new universe. The baby universe was filled with all His divine qualities and was charged with divine energies in fulfillment of God's Master plan to produce a super cosmic entity capable of producing human beings in due course.

The zygote, the first fertilized cell of the cosmos, started multiplying at an unprecedented speed, causing a rapid expansion of the total mass. It was this growth process and expansion, which human scientists probing the Universe, 15 billion years later from Planet Earth saw as the expanding Universe. As the consciousness and knowledge level of the scientists were limited to three dimensions, they were unable to understand the nature of the divine creation or cosmo-genesis, which operated at a multidimensional level, hidden from their view. The scientists were compelled to ascribe the cause of the expansion of the universe, which was due to a natural biological process, to an imaginary physical explosion, which they erroneously called the Big Bang. This error needs to be put right.

Although human scientists with their limited three-dimensional vision were unable to see the Universe as a living entity born of God, it was in reality a part of God. Further all living beings within the universe, including human beings, were also parts of God. All living entities continued to be in constant communication with God and with each other.

I must repeat that I have used the word God here to mean the totality of cosmic intelligence and life, which is common to all belief systems, and not to any anthropomorphic being which is specific to any particular religion. It could be substituted by any other word such as Dharma,

Chi, Allah, Brahman, Tao or simply Nature, which is the meaning of the word Dharma used by Buddhists. In accordance with the plans formulated by the Creator before and at cosmo-genesis, the growing universe started expanding and grew both in size and complexity forming an organic multifunctional complex. Galaxies were produced by the rapid expansion of the zygotic mass by the condensation of clouds of energy, which led to the crystallization of masses of energy that formed quasars and suns. The solar system evolved from our galaxy Milky Way about 10 billion years after Cosmo-genesis. Galaxies in due course produced clusters of stars within themselves. Our sun is one'such star. Fragments of the sun formed the planets, including earth. What inspired me to construct my own scenario, which I called cosmo-genesis, was my inability to accept that our Universe could come into being as the result of a powerful explosion, with no connection to any higher intelligence. Further no scientist has provided any direct evidence for the Big-Bang theory other than as an imagined corollary to the theory of the Expanding Universe. My scenario has provided a substitute to the big-bang theory for those who feel averse to it. The hypothesis that the Expansion of the Universe was generated by the Big-Bang needs to be changed to read that the Expansion of the Universe was generated by a process of cosmo-genesis parallel to a human birth and subsequent growth. Edgar Mitchell, Apollo astronaut, the founder of the International Organization of Noetic Sciences seeing earth from space while on a space flight experienced an altered state of consciousness and exclaimed: · "The whole cosmos is a living, dynamical being. The universe is not just a clockwork mechanism – creativity has been built in. It is always changing, dynamic. It is evolving into more complexity and more richness and more beauty all of the time. I suddenly realized it is all one, that this magnificent universe is a harmonious, directed, purposeful whole; that we humans, both as individuals and as a species are an integral part of the ongoing process of creation".

This scenario is in total conformity with the knowledge I received through three revelatory experiences, which are my cosmic consciousness experience, the chakra activation and my Near Death Experience, all of which have been explained in previous chapters. In fact the whole rationale for writing this book has been to share my worldview, which was formulated on the basis of the inspirational knowledge I had received. I firmly believe that the universe, as well as all its constituent parts, is made up of living entities. All of them are fully integrated, just as all chips in a computer are fully integrated.

It is indeed very interesting to note that Sir Fred Hoyle, who has been given the credit for coining the word Big Bang, did not himself believe it to be a scientifically proved fact. He had explained very clearly that he used the word Big Bang only in a critique of the Big Bang theory, and that he never supported the theory. There may have been other reasons why Sir Fred Hoyle was adamant that he did not want to associate himself with the Big Bang theory just because his colleagues did. I see the Big Bang theory as a way of destroying the positive image of the human being, which prevailed for centuries as having been created in the image of God. It strikes a blow at the position of honor and dignity traditionally enjoyed by just being human. Another argument against the plausibility of the Big Bang theory is that, as I have mentioned earlier a Big Bang could not have taken place in a void before any matter was created. As such, the Big Bang of the scientists was not a valid explanation for the expansion of the Universe. Thus, I am unable to believe in the Big-Bang theory for which I have not found any scientific evidence. I myself was an ardent believer in the Big Bang theory at one time and had much difficulty in deciding to review it critically.

After deciding to substitute the Big Bang theory by my scenario of cosmo-genesis, I could see how much of damage had already been done to the growing minds of present-day youth who are made to believe in a false theory regarding the origin of the universe. Any theory of the beginning of the Universe as a part of a complete worldview is bound to have a deep impact on the way of thinking of a person. For example, a child who discovers that he or she is a descendent of a great artist is bound to come to like art and even be drawn to choose art as a career. Likewise, a sensitive child who learns that the beginning of all life was caused by a mighty explosion called the Big Bang is likely to be drawn to join a gang or be subconsciously drawn to big explosions. Could this be one of the reasons why so many young people today are drawn to fighting and warfare and other acts of violence? They can be justified for thinking so because their origin as a living being was associated with a violent explosion. The words and impressions that come to my mind when I reflect on the Big Bang are destruction, violence, and cruelty, lack of order and discipline and similar negative images. As Big Bang stands for violence and hatred, it is the opposite of love and compassion. Big Bang stands for ugliness as against beauty and art. It is the antitheses of everything that is taught in religion such as prayer and meditation for which the required qualities are peace, quiet, serenity and silence. In short, it is the opposite of everything I live for and wish to include in this book, which I call Why I live. This explains why I find it difficult to agree with the Big Bang theory. We are desperately in need of a new creation story which could give young people a sense of pride and honor to live as humans, able to provide a positive answer to my question Why I Live?

Knowledge of the universe expanded rapidly as a result of the research of astronomers. Originally, the earth was thought to be stationary while heavenly bodies such as the sun, moon and the stars moved around the earth. Scientists like Kepler and Galileo devoted their lives to research, which led to the expansion of knowledge about the Universe. More recent scientists brought in evidence of the concept of inertia while Isaac Newton discovered working of the force of gravity. In 1916, Einstein formulated the general theory of relativity and in 1929, Hubble discovered the expansion of the Universe. While mathematically reversing the process of expansion of the universe to estimate the age of the universe, the assumption that any such convergence of matter had to generate immense heat and density, led the scientists to assume erroneously that a Big Bang is the best explanation of the initiating cause of a process of expansion as observed by Hubble. To me there is no better analogy than human anatomy and physiology to understand the cosmic web of life. Each human being or any other living entity is a living cell in the body of God. This is the essence of the message I received in my cosmic-consciousness experience. In the same way that the life of the body is dependent on the cell, the cell depends on the body for its sustenance. The seven functional systems of the body is a miracle of systemic order. Each cell is at all times in communication with every other cell. It opens the possibility of all entities working in harmony and generating synergy. It is on this basis that I formulated the cosmo-genesis scenario on the parallel of a biological conception of the universe, as an affirmation that God created the universe foreboding the sexual reproduction practice of the future living beings.

After discussing worldview and cosmogenesis, we have to move to the inevitable questions, what are our obligations as human beings and what are we able to do. In this quest we need to be led by the realization that we have an organic link with the universe, and all its parts. We use the word cosmos for the totality of existence, including all dimensions and all types of energy manifestations discussed above. The universe is that part of the cosmos which we can experience as human beings by physical means. As our bodies are three dimensional, what we can experience physically is limited to the three dimensions. What is the reality about the world we are living in? What is expected of a human being?

It is a pity that most of us humans have no understanding of our being an organic part of the universe. Although our knowledge of the universe is increasing daily we are unable to feel our true relationship with the universe, with the result that we have no affectionate feeling for our mother universe, thereby closing the doors to a most valuable influx of higher energy capable of giving us health, vitality and spiritual well being. Think of a man owning a big multi-story castle but occupying only a small room in the basement with only one's small window to allow air and sunlight in. If we do not recognize and enjoy our true relationship to the universe and the world we would not be any different from such a man.

When we consider our planet earth in relation to the entire universe, it is almost as insignificant in size as a particle of dust in a large building. Our world is deeply embedded within the universe. As in a complex system of computer hardware, the degree of importance of a part cannot be determined by its size. In the previous chapter I explained how in my cosmic consciousness experience I came to realize that the universe is a living entity and that all its constituent parts too are living entities. Modern scientists are slowly but gradually accepting this view. Gaia hypothesis has already gained wide popularity. I believe that the universe, which constitutes the physical structure of the cosmos, consists of a mind with intellectual faculties and emotions, comparable to a human being. All living parts of the cosmos such as galaxies, suns, planets and living beings are alive and similarly constituted. As human beings we should find it easy to understand and benefit from this relationship that is similar to our relationship with the cells in our body, on which we depend for our survival. It is a symbiotic relationship as cells on their part depend on us for their survival. The heart pumps fresh blood through arteries to regenerate the cells with oxygen supplied by the lungs. Veins carry damaged cells back to the heart for recycling. Nerves bring and carry messages to and from the brain keeping the cells supplied with vital information required for life supporting activities and survival.

This type of relationship exists between holons (parts of wholes) at all different levels of the holarchy (hierarchy of holons), enabling life within different levels of the cosmos to function smoothly and meaningfully. Each level of the holarchy is fully integrated and coordinated like thousands of integrated chips in a computer, enabling the grandeur of cosmic functioning, described in Hinduism as the dance of Shiva. Each of us is a living element or holon in the body of our magnificent cosmos.

We now know that the universe came into being through the creativity and will of God. Different kinds of crystals and rocks formed the physical foundation or skeletal structure of the baby universe. The first physical products of cosmogenesis would have been atoms and primitive cells. They evolved into more and more advanced forms as needed at different stages of growth. The first organic forms of new growth would have been galaxies, in the spiral arms of which stars started to form, and they became the suns with solar systems around them. Planets of different sizes appeared and with time produced mono-cellular and multicellular organisms on their surface, which evolved into millions of life forms including bacteria and primitive life. This was the beginning of life in the universe, including planet earth. Continental drifts on planets formed a moving stage for the evolution of more and more advanced life forms including human beings on earth. Arthur Clark s imaginative science fiction movie "2001 – Space Odyssey" contains imagery of lower animals such as apes being helped by divine intelligence to take the difficult quantum leap of evolving into human beings. This Means that we need the guidance and support of Higher intelligence to proceed on the path towards our destination.

Human beings who appeared comparatively recently used their power of thought and imagination to transform the earth into a paradise of beauty through the creative use of physical, emotional, intellectual and spiritual energies. These processes of creation are continuing not only within our planet, our solar system, our galaxy and our universe, but also through out the entire cosmos. As scientists have accepted the existence of more than one universe, we have to rename the universe as multiverse.

There is no doubt that God the Almighty with His incomparable creative abilities keeps on creating universes of other dimensions, which are beyond our reach. In Buddhism thousands of heavens with different space and time dimensions co-exist and enable beings to be born in other heavens in the process of reincarnation. Our problem is the narrowness of our vision. Because of the rules of perspective we see vast galaxies as small clouds, even smaller than ourselves. We need to make an effort to cultivate an undistorted global vision. The first steps of removing such distortions are through cultivating relevant mental skills such as self-remembering and meditation.

To fulfill our mission we must be aware of our rightful place in the cosmos and of all resources at our command. This chapter started with my scenario of how the universe came into existence. I called it cosmo-genesis; accepting the beginning of the universe and the origin of the cosmos as a divine birth, without deviating from the normal way in which a new life comes into existence. The need for understanding the worldview and our organic relationship to everything that exists is to enable us to fulfill our responsibilities towards the earth and the cosmos.

The earth is a spaceship and it is the responsibility of human beings, as the most intelligent beings living on earth, to guide it in the right direction as indicated to us by higher intelligence, which some may call divine omniscience or divine wisdom. In taking the responsibility to manage and guide planet earth to its destination three things are necessary. The first is the preservation and maintenance of the resources of planet earth; the second is ensuring peace so that we do not waste earth resources on unnecessary fighting & warfare; and the third is the proper sharing of resources among all living beings to ensure the prosperity of all beings by eliminating poverty. There is no need for poverty as planet earth has all the resources required to satisfy the needs of the entire humanity. The problem is that we have not yet been able to develop a system of administrative machinery capable of such a task. If planetary resources are properly shared through a proper distribution of wealth by a democratic world government, then only could all human beings who have the responsibility to guide spaceship earth to its destination have an equal share in the task. The cosmos itself is a large space ship being guided by a team of pilots at super human levels, of which our planet is one part. Human beings on planet earth should recognize that they belong to this team of pilots. It is essential for human beings to recognize their true relationship with the planet and with the entire cosmos. What I am referring to here is not just an academic knowledge of astronomy but also a true sense of our belonging to the earth and the entire cosmos. Let me give an analogy. A child separated from the mother for a long time during a time of war receives a letter with the mother's picture. Although this gives the child some idea of the mother, it is a very limited knowledge. The warm embrace the child receives when the mother and child are finally united is what is comparable to the true awareness of belonging. This is the nature of the awareness of belonging to the universe that we need to cultivate, so that we could perform all our responsibilities relating to our lives, our planet earth, and the cosmos to which all of us belong with a genuine feeling of love. Thomas Berry in his classic book "Dream of the Earth" discusses the need for a proper and meaningful creation story, which alone is able to give true meaning to human life and the nature of our relationship to planet earth.

All of us, together with all entities in the entire cosmos are parts of the one reality, which we call the cosmos or God. The cosmos is alive and has all characteristics of a living being. This bigger life to which we belong is spread out in all space, as life is present everywhere from a particle of dust to a human being, planet earth and all other cosmic entities. Although most of us know this, only very few of us have a true feeling of organically belonging to our planet earth and the universe.

The universe and its components are made up of four types of energy, called the four elements by ancient alchemists. They are earth, signifying physical energy; water for indicating emotional and aesthetic energy; air for denoting mental or

intellectual energy, and fire, for specifying supra-
mental or spiritual forces. These life energies that
represent different types of manifestations are
present everywhere at every level. Each of the four
types of energy has three modes of manifestation
according to the nature of activity it is engaged in
at any given time.

The three modes of energy manifestation are:

i   Creation, parallel to anabolism in a living
organism, as exemplified by the digestive
function which transforms the food we eat to
blood, which is a higher type of material.

ii Regulation, stabilizing and balancing of
energy, parallel to homeostasis in a human
body, which maintains the correct balances
such as that of glucose and other elements in
the blood; and

iii Utilization or using up of energy for diverse
purposes for meaningful activity and happiness,
parallel to katabolism.

The Hindu trinity illustrates the harmonious
operation of these three energies within the
Brahman or Godhead, in the symbolism of the
three constituent deities, as i. Brahma, ii. Vishnu
and iii. Shiva.

As each of the four types of energy manifest in three modes, there are twelve energy manifestation modes, all of them equally important for life.

In astrology the twelve signs of the zodiac signify these twelve manifestations of energy as follows:

		Earth	Water	Air	Fire
Creative	(Cardinal)	Capricorn	Cancer	Libra	Aries
Stabilizing	(Fixed)	Taurus	Scorpio	Aquarius	Leo
Utilization	(Mutable)	Virgo	Pisces	Gemini	Sagittarius

It is useful to understand these patterns of manifestation of life energy, to determine what action we might have to take with the resources at our disposal to optimize their benefits not only for living purposeful lives, but also to contribute to growth at all cosmic levels.

While reflecting on the purpose of life for answering the question Why I Live, let us start by examining our resources for fulfilling our obligations in the life process. I give below some of my thoughts about the resources at our disposal and possible methods of their utilization for the work we are required to do in living a purposeful and meaningful life. Let us survey our resources under the four categories Physical (earth), Emotional (water), intellectual or mental (air) and spiritual (fire). Only a few important issues can be discussed here. Gurdjieff taught the need for the balanced and integrated development of these four elements by using his favorite analogy of a carriage. The carriage has four components, each of them parallel to one of the four elements; (1) the body of the carriage (earth physical), (2) the horse (water feelings, emotions and motivations), (3) the driver (air mental faculties), (4) the owner (fire spiritual, links with the Creator). The body of the carriage has to be strong enough to last the journey. Horses are full of energy and want to keep running. The driver representing mental power has to be able to hold the reins, to guide the horses in the desired direction. The owner who alone knows the right way guides the driver to complete the journey to the destination. The lesson of the analogy is that each of the four elements has to be properly developed in every individual to lead a balanced and successful life. This applies to a single individual as well as to the total human tribe. This analogy is meaningful at this stage of our discussion for providing a basic outline for deliberation.

Another model which could make it easy to understand the pattern of integration of the four elements is by considering the cosmos as a giant computer, multimedia and communication complex in which all parts are fully integrated with each other.

Earth	hardware and resource section
Water	multimedia and music section
Air	memory, data processing and artificial intelligence center
Fire	communication center

Before ending the book let us now review our obligations for the future under these four headings.

Earth: – This element represents physical energies and activities undertaken for material benefit, including wealth and consolidation of power. As food, clothing and shelter are the essential needs for survival, an equitable distribution of wealth and resources is the basic requirement and characteristic of a civilized society. Human society is growing more and more complex due to the rapid growth of political institutions, scientific research and ever increasing speed of communication, paving the way for vast aggregations of resources and data. In the face of the ensuing accumulation of wealth and power in the modern world, the position of the individual is fast diminishing. Large corporations and other accumulations of power and wealth are progressively threatening individual welfare and peace of mind. It is extremely difficult to check this unhealthy tendency within a short period of time. There is a need to search for innovative solutions. Only effective grassroots level participatory organizations could enable individuals to feel that they can contribute at least in some measure for the benefit of their community. This alone can give meaning to their existence.

I was associated with a non-government institution in Sri Lanka called Sarvodaya, which proved to be well geared to counteract patterns of domination by giant organizations through fostering grassroots level participatory organizations. Sarvodaya brought together traditional knowledge of appropriate technology without ignoring modern science for sustainable development. For those who are interested in learning more about Sarvodaya, this institution maintains a website to provide information about its philosophy and activities. While working as a Training Officer in the Sri Lanka Institute of Development Administration, I arranged for all new recruits to the Administrative Service who were being trained to hold senior positions in government organizations, to visit the Sarvodaya Center and meet and discuss with the founder Dr. Ariyaratna, whose contributions to community services were recognized by many international awards including the coveted Ramon

Magsaysay award. One of the basic themes was the need to create self-reliance amongst the people by building up strong rural communities capable of bringing together traditional knowledge and modern science for sustainable development at community, national and global level.

A number of similar institutions in different countries such as Bhoodan in India, Kibbutz in Israel have at different times devised measures for promoting community involvement with different degrees of success. More recently a number of development agencies funded by developed countries or international agencies stepped into the field to support the concept of participation through non-government organizations (NGOs) in developing countries. Some national agencies with which I associated in some of the countries I visited in the course of my work are the United States Agency for International Development, (USAID), Canadian International Development Agency (CIDA), Swedish International Development Agency (SIPU) and the Commonwealth Fund for International Development. International agencies like the United Nations Development Program and the World Bank too contributed by supporting the NGOs. The United Nations Development Program (UNDP) defined grassroots participation as a process whose objective is to enable people to initiate action for self-reliant development and acquire the ability to influence and manage change within their society. Although non-government organizations have contributed immensely through funding, common people often lacked a feeling of direct identity with the NGOs, to the extent that organizations like Sarvodaya could generate. While ensuring measures for citizen participation through such participatory institutions at the grassroots level, each country needs a well-devised local government system to enable participation at the smallest village to progressively larger areas. Rural councils or city councils may be embedded in and controlled by counties, which are within states, which in turn are controlled by the Federal or National Governments.

Every country needs a well integrated hierarchy of local government and administrative machinery for an efficient administration. Each nation state has to device its own machinery combining efficiency and awareness of the needs and aspirations of the people. It is extremely important to recognize the gaps in the machinery, e.g. where some politicians and high level administrators become insensitive to rural development, local government and administrative machinery.

Most important of all, there are critical areas of decision-making and problem solving that are outside the scope of national governments. The

United Nations and its subsidiary institutions cannot be considered to be at the top of this hierarchical political and administrative complex covering the whole world, because the UN came into existence as a stopgap multinational advisory device at the end of the Second World War. It has done a remarkable job with all its limitations. However, there is a crying need to critically examine its institutional complex with a view to its fullest integration with the political and administrative machinery covering the whole world. Let us examine in brief the possibility of setting up a democratically elected world government responsible for the welfare of the entire world population.

World Government

In my opinion, one of the most important functions of a government is to ensure the equitable distribution of wealth among the different countries and their citizens. The purpose of democracy is obtaining the maximum participation of people in the government process. An efficient and fair government should be able to balance these two factors so that over accumulation of wealth does not negate popular participation.

We know that large countries like USA and India, which now have strong central governments, started a few centuries ago with thousands of unintegrated and independent principalities. In most countries, the process of territorial unification has been extremely difficult.

Today the earth has shrunk so much into a global village due to advanced communication systems, that the possibility of a democratically elected world government is quite evident. Computer technology is sophisticated enough to create databases capable of storing all categories of information about each human being even in one machine. Today the idea of a democratic world government, or democratic globalization has many proponents. They aim towards making people closer and more united, and want the world government to cover not only economic and political issues, but also other fields of activity and knowledge, giving world citizens a democratic access and a say in global activities beyond the legitimate purview of national governments. The administrative structure of the United Nations Office and Specialized Agencies can easily be brought together to form the basic infrastructure for a World Government Center. Considerable action has already been taken to study the legal and other implications involved in creating the required administrative structures and how such plans could be implemented. The movement towards setting up a democratic World Government has already started as evidenced by the vast volume of relevant research material found in the Internet. However the transition from national governments to a unitary world government is an extremely complicated process due to the fact that powerful national governments are likely to obstruct such a change, as it could reduce their position of power. It is necessary to make the process of change very methodical and very gradual. To start with, it would be necessary to set up a limited number of global or multinational organizations to manage different problem areas that are widely accepted as crucial and are common to more than one country.

Considering the urgent need to start action on these pressing issues, which cannot be postponed till the setting up of a world government, relevant multinational organizations need to be constituted immediately. In the long term, these organizations could federate to form the nucleus of a world government, whose functions and powers could gradually be expanded and consolidated.

A short list of some crucial areas suitable for setting up such interim international task forces and organizations are given below:

1. In order to provide prompt relief in the event of major natural disasters such as earthquakes, floods or tornadoes, which the governments of the affected areas may not be able to handle, a world body with trained personnel, specialized equipment and transport systems is needed to initiate immediate relief action, thereby saving lives and property.

2. Devising measures for integrating healing systems e.g. allopathy, homeopathy, naturopathy, ayurveda, acupuncture, chiropractic, flower essences, music therapy etc. all of which should be scientifically examined and included in the syllabuses of all medical schools, to avoid unfair discrimination due to ignorance. There are many other areas for concern like the possible abuse of genetic engineering and new health technologies similar to nanotechnology, which cannot be controlled by any one country.

3. The control of nuclear research and production of atomic weapons is a task which could be accomplished only by a world government agency, because it could never be handled effectively by one or a few nations which may already be involved in it. Although super powers have been negotiating and planning for cessation of nuclear testing and reductions

in nuclear arsenals since the mid-1950s, there have been very little or no success so far. It would appear that the delay is mostly due to their heart being not really in it. An international body with sufficient power and authority needs to be set up immediately.

4. A global authority for controlling indiscriminate mining and extraction of non-renewable earth and ocean resources like gas and precious metals is long overdue. We also need systems for taxing of national incomes from countries, which engage in illicit exploitation of such nonrenewable resources, according to the volume of earnings. Income from such measures could be a major source of income for running the world government.

5. In the area of space exploration, many controversial decisions such as the setting up of national or international space stations will need to be monitored by a world government.

6. In the field of education, global policy-making and setting up of guidelines is needed to coordinate the planning of education, with a view to the future development needs of mankind. The syllabuses should be expanded to include the most recent scientific discoveries,

as well as the world heritage of the essence of ethical and religious knowledge, including traditional knowledge and skills.

This list is only a sample, as there are many other important areas needing urgent attention.

Concerning all these areas, only an enlightened and impartial leadership group could start taking action to satisfy the needs of the future world, which are even beyond our imagination at this stage. What is needed at the outset is the setting up of a global think tank representing all interests and including the best scientists and thinkers, legal experts, historians, metaphysicians etc. who would be entrusted with the task of studying all the introductory studies and spadework done'so far in this field, brainstorming for innovative solutions and making firm proposals which could be referred to Universities and Legal experts, and other concerned groups for formulating solid plans and implementation programs for the necessary changes.

We end here our discussion concerning the earth element, which signifies power, wealth and participation, the major part of which had to be devoted to the desirability of setting up a world government, as a necessary step in the advancement of human culture and civilization.

The WATER element covers areas of action, which are designated as emotions or feelings and are not directly related to the means of physical survival. The power of love is the highest manifestation of the water element.

This area covers emotional resources, to which we are drawn by higher faculties seeking harmony with satisfactions of a non-material nature, exemplified by music and the arts. The ideal is the manifestation of positive emotions, as a means of generating love and happiness, which are the fundamental goals of existence. Stimulating and expressing positive emotions can activate dynamic energy systems of the body. One of the best expositions on the significance of developing positive emotions is the Natya Sastra, a spiritual treatise written in India by the sage Bharatha around the sixth century before Christ, to which all forms of Indian classical art forms including dance and drama attribute their origin, theory and technique. It is regarded as the fifth Veda, as it primarily endeavors to establish the Divine origin of the arts and their sacredness. According to this treatise Brahma the creator, created this art called Natya, taking literature from the Rig Veda, music from the Sama Veda, abhinaya or histrionics from the Yajur Veda and Rasa or aesthetic experience from the Atharva. Natya Sastra is a comprehensive exposition encompassing every aspect of aesthetic expression including dance, drama, music, poetics and literature. The nine emotions, according to classical Indian treatises on the performing arts, are Love and Sex, Humor, Sorrow, Anger, Courage, Fear, Disgust, Surprise, and Harmony. These nine emotions are considered to be the raw material for producing works of art through which human beings can reach highest ecstasy enabling harmony with the divine, being one of the major objectives of human life. Centralized research is needed into principles of traditional and classical music and the arts, including their metaphysical basis.

There are many levels of art and music. At the lower level they put you to sleep. At higher levels they can awaken you. At the highest level of objective art, they can be utilized as a tool to achieve any desired goals including healing, spiritual development and promotion of peace.

Scholars who have done advanced research into principles of classical music have discovered hidden principles of objective sound. Objective sound is the key to the use of sound or music to obtain predetermined results such as healing. According to a story from India, when an angry Veena player produced fire by playing a negative combination of notes, another musician played a different combination of notes to produce rain to put off the fire. Gurdjieff once demonstrated objective sound by sitting at the piano and writing some words on a paper, which he folded and put on a table to be seen by everyone. After playing some music he requested one of the listeners to read his note. It mentioned the name of some one present in the audience, who was then called on to the stage and was asked to read the note. It mentioned that the spectator would find a blister on his right leg, and on examining his leg was surprised to find a blister exactly as described. As Gurdjieff played a few more notes on the piano the blister vanished to the amazement of everybody. In Ouspensky's book In Search of the Miraculous Gurdjieff's principles of objective sound and objective music are more fully explained. It says that objective music can obtain not only physical, but also psychological and spiritual manifestations. It says that art and music are not only means of entertainment, but also tools for more serious results when used by some one with the correct knowledge. It is still a hidden art and another area in which research is much needed.

Air

Air represents the power of thought, which is the most essential faculty of human life. For those who recognize that we are a microcosm of the Macrocosm that is at the apex of all life, whether you call it the cosmos, God, or whatever other name according to your worldview, we as human beings represent the divine attribute of omniscience.

Thought is the principle manifestation of consciousness. Intelligence is a measure of thought power, which can be cultivated by education. Our power of thought is an immensely potent tool. Let us devote this section to understand our responsibilities in the areas of thought and education to fulfill our obligations to the world of tomorrow. Case studies have demonstrated that outcomes of positive thinking and negative thinking are astonishing. Knowledge relating to effective systems of thinking is easily available from recent writers such as Deepak Chopra and Edward de Bono. De Bono's writings on lateral thinking, on which the technique of brainstorming was based, is essential reading for anybody interested in this field. Ancient Huna teachings of Hawaii on the potential of guided thinking are amazing. They teach that any thought that passes through the mind is invariably materialized, whether they are a wish, a fear or an aversion, which means that utmost care is needed to keep thoughts well under control. What believers of Huna teachings of Hawaii achieve through guided thinking is awesome. I was fascinated to read and practice publications by Kahlil Serge based on Hawaiian philosophy, which are freely obtainable through the Internet. Thought control is the basic path to effective meditation. Buddhist teaching is almost entirely based on the use of right thinking in life.

If we are concerned for the welfare of future generations, we have to improve the quality of education by taking firm steps to advance the content as well as the techniques of education. There is good hope for utilizing computer and TV based education as computers are getting faster and more powerful, so that one good teacher can reach virtually all students in the world. As discussed in the previous chapter where possibilities of a world government were explored, the future of education is an area that should be handled by a group of world experts. Knowledge that is expanding rapidly could have been made available through the expanding internet networks, if not for ever tightening copyright restrictions. There is a war going on between those standing for an open door policy or privatization for education material, as against others seeking commoditization of knowledge through copyright restrictions. There is hope for keeping the doors open with the Massachusetts Institute of Technology's bold experiment called Open Courseware Initiative in which one of the world's leading universities is making its teaching material accessible on the Internet, free of charge, to any user anywhere in the world. As discussed in the previous chapter where possibilities of a world government were explored, the future of education is an area, which should be handled by a group of world experts with worldwide recognition who can plan for a golden era of education in the next few decades. (http://ocw.mit.edu/index.html) To ensure enlightened education systems for future generations, we need to blend all the best of world knowledge in constructing educational curricula for future generations. A good example is the educare concept of Sathya Sai Baba being presently tried out in India, in which the latest scientific knowledge is blended with the essence of teachings from ancient scriptures such as the Vedas. We have to be thankful to pioneers in the field of education who have contributed to improving our systems of education through their enlightened thinking. Although opinions vary, a few memorable names are Jan Komensky or Comenius, John Locke, Jean Jacques Rousseau, Johann Heinrich Pestalozzi, Friedrich Froebel, Herbert Spencer, John Dewey, Maria Montessori, Jean Piaget and Ivan Illich. Those who are interested may refer the internet or relevant books for details.

Power of the internet needs to be recognized as the prototype of the global and subsequently the galactic prototype of an integrated information infrastructure. If its properties are not explored and planned by the most competent authorities and controlled by a world body it could fall into wrong hands and cause great damage for future society.

Fire

Fire, which is the fourth element, represents the owner of the carriage, which in this analogy is my innermost self, as well as the Higher Cosmic Being of which I am a living cell. All living entities are living organs of this Higher consciousness. As a cell of the totality, I am entrusted with certain specific functions and roles, which are essential to my life, as well as to the entire cosmic life. At lower levels of self development we may not even be fully aware of these roles. To understand more precisely what these roles are, let us review the analogy of the carriage, because it explains in a simple way the nature of the four elements and how they are integrated. In this analogy the Earth element symbolizes the body of the carriage including all the tools and physical resources. It represents one's body with all the resources needed to sustain life. If the carriage is not strong and not well maintained, it might not last the journey. If the horses, representing motivation, are not strong and not well trained they will not be able to draw the carriage to the end of the journey. If the driver, representing mental faculties, is not healthy and awake, he will not be able to hold the reins skillfully to get the horses to pull the carriage along the road and complete the journey. The driver has to be diligent to follow the instructions of the owner who alone knows the destination. Luckily the owner, representing Higher Intelligence, knows when and how to repair the cart, feed the horses and heal the driver. What we need is to be able to integrate all four elements and have faith in the master and as trustworthy children of the master do what is necessary to make the journey safe and happy for all of us. The master is what we generally call God. We need to have faith in Him and follow His instructions. When He manifests His love by acting directly to save us from a calamity, we call it synchronicity. I have faith in Him and that is WHY I LIVE. We have been taught that the main attributes of God are omnipotence, omniscience and omnipresence. I have suggested that we include Omni loving to the Omni attributes of God. Expressing and manifesting genuine love is the starting point. Love towards all living beings is best expressed by improving our behavior towards others. This is the fundamental principle of all divine teaching as expressed in different religious teachings. We as humans born in our planet Gaia have many responsibilities. How do we find out our responsibilities? Advice given by messengers of God is available to us in the scriptures, or the dharma as Buddhists call it. I mention below some of the main teachings arranged in chronological order. Details about these teachings are easily available in relevant books, the Internet or Encyclopedias. In 3000BC the Egyptian MAAT, which means code of behavior was formulated and written down, containing 42 laws or principles of behavior. About 1000 B. C. the ten commandments were revealed to Moses. According to ancient tradition the ten commandments are divided into two separate tablets: the first four on one tablet, stipulating one's duty to God and the last six on a second tablet, listing the duties to fellow humans. Around 500 BC Lord Buddha, who meditated in the jungle till he received enlightenment, revealed the four noble truths and the eightfold path. These are summarized in chapter 7. The first six of the eight guidelines are related to human behavior. The seventh is the cultivation of self-remembering and awareness. The eighth is meditation, which leads to merging with Higher Intelligence.

At the beginning of the Christian Era Jesus Christ taught the two golden rules in the following words. – "All things whatsoever ye would that men should do to you, do ye even so to them and Thou shalt love the Lord thy God with all thy heart, and with all thy soul, and with all thy strength, and with all thy mind; and thy neighbour as thyself." In the 6th century Mohammad who founded Islam received revelations which led to new articles of faith and tenets of behavior while also accepting the 10 commandments of Judaism as revealed to Moses.

In this way all religious teachers have taught very similar principles of behavior, which are preserved in their scriptures.

Multifarious programs of action are needed to promote the spiritual development of all beings, through whatever paths may be suitable for each of them. Normally the religion one is born into serves as the foundation. We have to utilize all the resources available e.g. all teachings and all practices leading to spiritual development. I have already discussed in the chapter on religions my belief that all major religions originated from one'source. We need not be reluctant to read and learn the teachings of other religions, thus paving the way for religious harmony. Interfaith cooperation movements should be supported and networked for global activity. The study of comparative religion needs to be encouraged in every possible way. We now have many Encyclopedias of Religion, which facilitate the study of comparative religion; to me one of the best is Mircea Eliade s Encyclopedia of Religion. Another growing nccd is thc compilation of scientific databases of the teachings of major religions. This is a major task which is best entrusted to a group of Universities.

Apart from the organizations of major religions of which I have written briefly in the previous chapters, the following are some of the present day organizations from which I received inspiration and assistance in my study of comparative religion. I am grateful to the University of Metaphysics founded and headed by Dr. John Leon Masters for assisting in my studies. For over 40 years, he has played a leading role in the field of Metaphysical research and teaching. It started in California and now has spread its activities to Nevada and Arizona. The Kundalini Research Network (KRN) of which I was a member and have presented papers at their research seminars, is worthy of special mention for their valuable contributions in research into kundalini energy and related spiritual transformations of consciousness. Institute of Noetic Sciences (IONS) founded by astronaut Edgar Mitchell (as mentioned earlier in Chapter 19) is worthy of mentioning as an organization that conducts and sponsors research into the potentials and powers of consciousness with a vision of human evolution with manifestations of higher consciousness. Its objectives include the extending of our understanding of human capacities, exploring the powers of consciousness and harnessing the powers of love and wisdom, out of which a globally conscious and compassionate civilization is bound to arise.

While I have acknowledged my indebtedness to Ken Wilber One Taste for the inspiration to continue writing this book, I am also deeply indebted to his books, journals and articles for the high quality of his contributions towards the merging together of the field of comparative religion and metaphysics with the latest developments in modern science. It is unfortunate that science and religion still operate from two different camps. There have been many ad-hoc attempts for the merging of the religious and scientific scenarios. One promising area has been in conducting scientific research into changes of energy frequencies, measured as alpha, beta, theta etc. during different types or stages of meditation. Such attempts need to be monitored and encouraged. The term neurotheology has sometimes been used for such studies. (For example, see the Newsweek article of 5/7/2001 on God and the Brain How – We're Wired for Spirituality.) The ultimate responsibility for the worldview and quality of life of the next generation rests squarely on human beings living today. It all depends on the role of each individual, acting separately or collectively. Each human being is uniquely responsible for the welfare of human beings of the future. Just as one's sick cell in a body can turn cancerous, and even kill the host body, the reverse is also true. Positive contributions of even one individual, generating group efforts and synergies, can save planet earth from impending disasters and ensure a future world of peace, prosperity and enlightenment. The way we live has an effect not only on our neighbors, and ourselves but also on Gaia and the whole cosmos. Each of us is carrying a great responsibility for the future of ourselves as well as the entire cosmos, of which we are an organic element. As the popular saying goes, "Be the change you wish to see."

Chapter 20

Why We Live – Lessons of Experience

What follows are key concepts based on my life experience of seventy-six years. These may be my answers to the question "What are the steps leading to a life devoted to self-development, as against living a normal life of stagnation?" What follows is a list of Eight Key words focusing on my worldview and a sequential code of behavior to reach the aspired goals.

Sincerity And Seriousness

At the starting point of stepping into the path of serious self-development, it is necessary to be sincere about one's decision and the intention to exit from the crowded freeway of normal self-centered behavior to the narrow path of altruism, kindness, love and spiritual development. A sincere desire to breakaway from this stagnation and regression, and devote at least some time for higher interests needs a sincere and serious determination. For those who are too deeply engrossed in the social life, humorously described as keeping up with the Joneses, there is no alternative to keep on driving along the crowded free-way, at least with some conscience. When it is proper time to make the change, when the signal comes from above, there will be no hesitation to take the exit. An example of total and abrupt change was demonstrated by Lord Buddha who left His palace with all its comforts and royal heritage to accept the suffering of jungle life for the sake of spiritual development. By so doing he opened a rational path of spiritual development for all mankind.

Smile

A genuine smile is an outer manifestation of one's love for humanity. It demonstrates the acceptance of the noble maxim of loving thy neighbor and recognizing the brotherhood of man. A smiling nature accompanied by inner happiness is an unmistakable sign of the initiation and activation of a process of inner growth. Strengthening our relationships with the community is the first requirement in the need to build up teams for fulfilling our responsibilities as care takers of the earth and the cosmos. A smile has the function of lubricating the social system, to eliminate inter-personal friction.

Self-remembering

Remembering oneself is the best way of clearing the mind of all unnecessary thoughts. For self-remembering effectively one needs to maintain one's awareness of oneself continuously and that needs considerable practice. Gurdjieff, who popularized this self-development technique, used the image of a double-headed arrow to explain self-remembering. Normal sensory awareness is like an arrow pointing from your mind to the object of perception. At that moment one is aware only of the object of perception, but not mindful of oneself. In self-remembering the arrow is double pointed, as one is aware of the object of perception as well as oneself, as the subject of the act of perception. This does not allow room for any other mental activity or thoughts. Gurdjieff maintained that the vast majority of people who think they are awake are in fact sleeping most of the time. Self-remembering is the technique he used to assist people to keep awake. I use the example of self-remembering here to represent a large number of mental disciplines which are used to bring the process of thinking under control. Prayer and meditation are the best means of spiritual and self-development. Higher intelligence (God) is always communicating to us what the right course of action is. The problem is our insensitivity and constant engagement of the mind on unnecessary diversions, which block communication. All serious aspirants of spiritual development need, not only to find at least one'such path of contemplation, but also practice it incessantly.

Share

Sharing is an unmistakable manifestation of love indicating a loosening grip of ego and greed, and needs to be practiced with neither discrimination nor restraint. Spontaneous giving can be practiced at any level, whether individual, organizational, community or institutional. At the community level we could share our resources so as to help other fellow beings. There is a crying need to eliminate poverty, which is the major cause for most of our problems. We need to devise more efficient machinery at different institutional levels for equitable distribution of wealth. What is stressed here is more relevant to sharing at the individual level with an element of sacrifice, rather than at impersonal and institutional levels.

Service

Individual acts of service and sacrifice for the benefit of others is the next step. Each of us is responsible for our own survival as well as for the welfare of our neighborhood, community, our planet earth and the entire cosmos. We as human beings, need a genuine feeling of belonging to planet earth, and protect its environment so that we can be of real service by eliminating all the current problems of planet earth, which have prevented it from being a peaceful planet. The word service also includes the concept of guiding all human beings into a future, which is marked by peace and prosperity.

Synergy

When two people each with five units of energy join to work as a team, their total energy is not ten, it could be hundred. The total energy of any team is far beyond the sum total of individual efforts. Therefore whenever we feel that a task needs enhanced group effort, team building is necessary.

It is advisable to join groups or associations, which are in agreement with our thinking and motives. If the situations demand it, we should always be prepared to volunteer for service and also to provide leadership, as there is always a need for committed leaders. The story of the 100th monkey, whether fact or fiction, is considered a good example of how the concept of synergy operates. Some monkeys living in a small island survived by eating yams, which grew by the waterside. One day one of them finding the taste of the mud offensive washed the yams impulsively. Another monkey who saw what happened followed suit. More and more monkeys started washing their yams. Suddenly the monkeys in the adjoining island too started washing their yams, although they had no direct contact or communication with the monkeys in the first island. The explanation is that when the number of monkeys washing their yams increased, the critical mass of synergy generated thereby was sufficient to transmit a powerful telepathic message to monkeys in the adjoining island, causing them to follow the same pattern of behavior. According to this way of thinking, any group action is able to generate a strong synergic force, which results in the propagation of a given pattern of behavior. The lesson to be learnt is that a change of behavior by a sufficiently large number of people in one place has the possibility of spreading far and wide even without any direct communication.

Synchronicity

Synchronicities are meaningful coincidences, in which there is unmistakable evidence of the working of a higher intelligence. Experiments have proved the benefits of increasing our awareness of such manifestations of higher intelligence. When combined with self-remembering they allow us to obtain proof of our belonging to a larger entity with higher intelligence. When an incident that can be classed as an example of synchronicity takes place, one has to direct one's attention to it with the intention of understanding the sequence of events. Take for example the incidents I have described in chapter 18. If we analyze the incident where I was saved from being attacked by a poisonous snake, it becomes very clear that some higher power has been observing and guiding the course of events while intervening at the most crucial moments. For example:

1. My falling asleep while reading a book in bed, without switching off the room lights as was usual;

2. My hearing the loud cry of a child, which could have been my daughters;
3. My getting up from sleep, and seeing the snake coming towards me;
4. Calling my wife to alert the neighbors;
5. My wife being able to call the neighbors in time for them to be able to come and capture the snake.

All these events had to take place in an incredibly short span of time for my life to have been saved. Such incidents have given me a strong belief that I am being constantly watched by God and saved in the event of danger. I consider my whole life to be an intensive training program custom-made for me and supervised by higher intelligences, for which I have used the collective term God. I know that it is according to God's wish that I have written this book to share my experiences with others who could benefit by reading about the various events in my life, which have served as lessons for me. Like cells in a living body, we are being scanned every millisecond by Higher Intelligences for our condition, thoughts, feelings, health and all circumstances. Therefore it takes no time for any required intervention. The more we understand how synchronicity works, we move closer to its divine source and there will be more and more synchronicities in our lives. Deepak Chopra calls this phenomenon synchro-destiny.

Spirituality

When we speak of body, mind and spirit we assume three types of energies, physical, mental and spiritual. Spiritual energies exist beyond both physical and mental domains. In other words we are unable to produce spiritual energies by physical or mental effort. Spiritual energy is made available to us as and when needed.

There is an old religious maxim that the teacher, representing the spiritual, appears only when the student is ready. What it means is that when we exert the right degree of effort by ourselves, divine grace will manifest without fail to assist us to fulfill our desires. The story of the cart-driver whose cartwheel was stuck in a muddy furrow illustrates this principle, which is common to all major religions. As the cart-driver felt that it was an impossible task for him to push the cart out of the mud by himself, he prayed to God and sat down to rest. He received no help and it was getting dark. He would not dare spend the night in this lonely place. In his desperation he put his shoulder to the wheel and started pushing with all his might. Then an old man appeared and pushed the other wheel and the cart came free. The cart-driver thanked him and asked him who he was. He replied, I am God to whom you prayed. I have been watching till you yourself started pushing your cart. For any successful accomplishment effort and grace are equally needed. As God is omniscient, omnipotent, omnipresent and all loving, there is nothing, which is impossible.

What I have presented in this book are some fragments of knowledge gained through my own life experience. I see them as tiny droplets of water in the vast ocean of higher knowledge, which is open to everybody. Exploring higher knowledge has been a great joy to me. I now close this book wishing dear readers all the blessings needed to fulfill their highest ambitions and be happy.

Amen!   Om!   Sadhu!

Appendix I

DETAILED CONTENTS— ANALYTICAL TABLE

PART ONE   MY LIFE

Chapter 1 My Childhood 1928-354 .... p19
About Sri Lanka. Portuguese, Dutch and British rule. Birth memories. Environment of books. Precocious Nature. Feeling of not belonging here. Cosmic Consciousness Experience. Bright light. Influx of Knowledge. Another dimension of Space & Time. Influence on my education. Having to live away from home. Saved from a poisonous snake.

Chapter 2 Education up to University Graduation 1935-1952 ....p27
Self study for the University Entrance Examination. University Studies. Success in Civil Service

Competitive Examination. Recruitment to the Administrative Service as an Assistant Commissioner of Local Government in the Ministry of Local government.

Chapter 3 Public Service in Sri Lanka
                1952-1975 .... p30
Training in Colombo. In Ratnapura-The gem mining area. Matale District. Attack by strange microscopic parasites in a jungle area. Dutch fortress of Galle. Founder Member of Junior Chamber Chapter. Transfer to Matara. Formation of a Subud Group. Visit of Bapak, Subud Founder. My marriage. Subud testing. Postgraduate studies in England. Recruitment to Institute of Development Administration. Training in Japan and Netherlands, etc.

Chapter 4 International Civil Service
                1975-1992 .... p50
United Nations Consultancy at CAFRAD, Morocco. Commonwealth Fund assignment in Botswana as Staff Development & Training Officer. About Botswana. Bushmen of the Kalahari.

Chapter 5 In USA. Retirement p61
Metaphysical studies & research. Lecture at Kundalini Research Convention in Toronto. Univ.

of Metaphysics—Masters and Doctoral degrees. Lectures at annual Conventions. Started website "Why live". Meditation progress – Belonging to the Universe as against knowledge of the Universe. Life at Fickett Towers.

PART TWO   VENTURES WITH TEACHERS AND TEACHINGS

IIA Different Paths to Self-Development .... p69 The significance of the religion one is born into. Syncretism. Guidelines to explore one's own religion and other religions. Finger pointing to the moon. Relevant sayings of spiritual teachers. Benefits of learning esoteric teachings . Parable of the airplane.

Chapter 6 Hinduism – The cosmos as a
            living entity.............................. p81
Originated from Vedas of 4000 years ago. The cosmos as a living being. Functions of the Hindu Trinity: Brahma (anabolism) Vishnu (homeostasis), Shiva (katabolism). Their consorts. Henotheism. Different Yogas including meditation, Kundalini energy and chakras. Goal of Sat-Chit-Ananda.

Chapter 7 Buddhism–Enlightenment
        by one's own effort p84
*Four Noble Truths. The Eightfold Path. Theravada
or Hinayana Buddhism, Mahayana or Zen
Buddhism and Vajrayana or Tibetan Buddhism.*

Chapter 8 Christianity–Salvation by
        divine guidance & grace p87
*Jesus Christ, Son of God. Love God and thy neighbor
equally. Esoteric teachings e.g. Philokalia. Thomas
Merton exploring other religious paths.*

Chapter 9 Islam p90
*Founder Mohammed in Arabia 7th century.
My personal contacts with Islam in Sri Lanka,
Morocco, Botswana and U.K. Five Pillars of Islam.
Sharia or Law. Mawlid and Miraj. Sufism.*

Chapter 10 Gurdjieff & Ouspensky.
        Waking up from sleep p93
*Admission to Gurdjieff Group through University
Dean. Gurdjieff work. Self-remembering as a
double-headed arrow. Awakening from sleep.
The Fourth Way. . Ray of Creation. Energy
Transformation methods.*

Chapter 11 Subud – Divine Guidance to Find the Right Path p98
"Concerning Subud" by J. G. Bennett, My First Latihan and Subud Testing. Beginning of Subud in Indonesia. Submission, Surrender, Sincerity & Patience. . My encounter with an adversary of Subud leads to an astonishing experience. Nature of worship that can make contact with the Great Life. Extract from the Founder's book.

Chapter 12 Sathya Sai Baba p106
Supernatural powers from childhood. Talks and Miracles attract large crowds. Encourages study and practice of all major religions. Rural birthplace transformed into an advanced township. Unique Hospital where heart surgery is free of cost. Number of devotees increasing rapidly. Believed to be the second of three consecutive avatars.

Chapter 13 Other Paths & esoteric groups of the main religions p108
Monastic Christianity, Sufism, Baha'i. Mention of Kabbalah and Tantra.

PART THREE MY SPIRITUAL EXPERIENCES

IIIA Some Landmarks in my spiritual development process

Chapter 14 Cosmic Consciousness
                 Experience p119
A beautiful morning. The beginning of a change process. A bright golden light. Changes in space and time dimensions. Feelings of love and joy. Influx of new knowledge. Divine presence. Awareness of belonging to the Cosmos. Difficulties of communicating with elders. Main elements of the experience. Impact on Education. Words holon and holarchy.

Chapter 15 Chakra Activation &
                 Kundalini Energy p130
Meditation to get rid of stress. Reading Vivekananda. Trying to slow down thinking process. Self-remembering. Group meditations. The location of chakras. Merging of chakras with holarchy levels. Chakras as Multi-functional energy centers. How chakras correspond with holarchy levels.

Chapter 16 Near Death Experience...........p146
Symptoms of Heart disease. Angiogram. By-Pass surgery successful. Heart attack and injury to Apex

Muscle. Doctors diagnosed critical state and used life-support. An announcement of death.. Moving towards a bright light through a dark tunnel.. I turn towards a smaller light on the side and see my wife praying. Floating in space side by side with her amidst beautiful scenery. I see myself in a healing temple, which I am told is Tibetan and planned to explore this path later. My reluctant return to my own body.

Chapter 17 Kataragama p153
Visiting a jungle shrine in South Sri Lanka. Feeling a strong spiritual energy. Learning about traditional beliefs about the shrine. Unusual spiritual practice involving physical endurances such as fire-walking. Miraculous experience of seeing revelatory words. Vortexes as Parallels of chakras.

Chapter 18 Other Remarkable
             Experiences p159
Timely appearance of Tow Truck
The book I needed desperately found in a trash bin
Spiritual GPS
Surgery Avoided
Car Stops by Itself to Save Child
Saved from a poisonous snake

Risorgimento
Using a Citroen Club Car saved our lives
Car expressing her feelings

PART FOUR   SYNTHESIS

IVA Introduction to Part IV
Expansion of the childhood worldview. Cosmic
Consciousness Experience. Gurdjieff work and
Subud. Personal experiences.

Chapter 19 My World View..........................p178
Worldview is one's total mental framework. My
belief in a supreme Higher Intelligence, which
may be called by any name, including God. God
as all loving. Creation as a work of art. A random
explosion cannot bring forth a universe filled
with intelligence? How God could have planned
to create the Universe. The three dimensional
universe could have been created by an omni
dimensional Higher Intelligence that we call God.
Seven dimensional holarchy of the Universe. Edgar
Mitchell's Enlightening vision on seeing Earth
from space. The difference between knowing and
belonging. Universe and its elements as living
beings. Atoms and cells. Suns and Planets. Arthur
Clarke's "2001-Space Odyssey" concept of guided
evolution. Buddhist cosmology. Self awareness

and time consciousness. Our obligations for the future of mankind and the cosmos, discussed under the four divisions of energy: earth, water, air and fire, explained through the analogy of the carriage.

Earth – desirability of a world government for equitable sharing of power and resources.

Need for grassroots level participatory organizations.

Water – for positive growth in the cultural and aesthetic activities through research needed to integrate different cultural traditions.

Air – for positive improvements in mental activity by sharing intellectual resources for improved educational systems through computers and multimedia techniques.

Fire – action for improving religious harmony by reviewing religious knowledge of different ages and promoting interfaith activities. Educational establishments promoting comparative religion and metaphysical studies need to be assisted and strengthened.

Chapter 20 Lessons of Life Experience....p228
Eight key steps to holistic development: Sincerity and Seriousness, Smiling, Self-remembering and meditation, Sharing, Service, Synergy, Synchronicity and Spirituality.

Appendix 2

SOME RECOMMENDED BOOKS

Aurobindo – The Life Divine and the Synthesis of Yoga – Centenary Library, Pondicherry

Bancroft, Anne (1978) Modern Mystics and Sages – Paladin

Bapak's (1975) SUSILA BUDHI DHARMA – Subud Publications International

Bateson, G. (1979) Mind and Nature – Dutton

Beierle, (1979) Autobiography of God

Bennett, J. G. (1965) Long Pilgrimage (Life and Teaching of ShivaPuri Baba) Hodder

Bennett, J.G. (1999 What Are We Living For – Bennett Books

Bennett, J. G. (1959)Concerning Subud Hodder & Stoughton(Publisher)

Bertalanffy, L. von (1968) General System Theory – Braziller, NY

Beversluis Joel Source Book of the World's Religions New World Library

Bucke, R Maurice 1900 COSMIC CONSCIOUSNESS – Arkana

Campbell, Joseph (1968) The Hero with a Thousand Faces – World NY.

Campbell, Joseph (1959) The Masks of God – Viking

Capra, F. (1991) Belonging to the Universe – Harper

Capra, Fritjof(1996) The Web of Life – Anchor

Casteneda, Carlos Teachings of Don Juan etc.

Chardin, Teilhard (1979) The Human Search – Fount paper Backs

Chopra, Deepak (2003) The Spontaneous Fulfillment of Desire – Harmony Books

Coestler, A. (1964) The Act of Creation – Dell, NY

Darwin, C. (1872) Origin of Species and the Descent of Man

De Silva Chandra, Richard (1987) Sri Lanka – A History – New Printindia Pvt Ltd.,

Effendi, Shoghi (1953) Guidance for Today and Tomorrow – Baha'i Publishing Trust

Eliade, Mircea (1986) Encyclopedia of Religion

Evans-Wentz, W. (1971) Tibetan Yoga and Secret Doctrines – Oxford Univ. London

Ferris, Timothy (1997) The Whole Shebang
– Simon & Schuster

Fromm, & Suzuki (1970) Zen Buddhism and
Psycho-Analysis – Harper

Gard, Richard (1962). Buddhism. NY: George
Braziller.

Greenwell, Bonnie (1990) Energies of Transformation
– Shakti river Press

Gurdjieff, G.I. (1950) All and Everything –
Dutton

Hall, Manly Palmer (1949) The Adepts of the
Western Esoteric Tradition – PRS

Harman, Willis (1998) Global Mind Change
– Noetic Sciences

Hawking, Steven W. (1988) A Brief History of
Time – Bantam

Herbert, Nick (1993) Elemental Mind – Dutton

Hobbes, T. (1990) The Leviathan – Prometheus
Books

Holroyd, Stuart (1989) Arkana Dictionary of New
Perspectives – Arkana

Huxley, A (1944) The Perennial Philosophy
– Harper and Row

James, W. (1901) The Varieties of Religious
Experience – Colliers N.Y.

Johari, Harish (1987) Chakras – Harper and Row

John of the Cross (1979) The Collected Works
– Kavanaugh

Jordan, Michael (1993) Encyclopedia of Gods
– Facts on file

Jsobi, J. (1942) The Psychology of C. J. Jung
– Routledge

Jung, C.V. (1957) The Undiscovered Self –
Mentor

Kafatos, M & Nadeau R.(1944) The Conscious
Universe – Sprnger-Verlag

Lama Yeshe (1987) Introduction to Tantra
– Wisdom Publications

Levin, Michal (2002)Meditation – D.K.Publishing

Lovelock, J. (1988) The Ages of Gaia – Norton
NY.

Maslow, (1970) Religions, Values and Peak
Experiences – Viking

Metzner, Ralph (1971) Maps of Consciousness
– Collier Books

Milarepa, (1999)The Hundred Thousand Songs
– Shambala

Monrioe, R. (1971) Journeys out of the body
– Double day NY.

Mookerjee, A. (1982) Kundalini – Destiny Books,
NY.

Narada (1975) A Manual of Abhidhamma
– Buddhist Publication Society, Kandy, Sri
Lanka

Needleman, Jacob (1970) The New Religions
– Double Day & Company

Needleman, Jacob (1974) The Sword of Knosis – Penguin

Nyanaponika (1973) The Heart of Buddhist Meditation–Weiser, NY

Ouspensky, P.D. (1950) In Search of the Miraculous – Routledge

Ouspensky, P.D. (1957) The Fourth Way – Random House

Ouspensky, P.D. (1971) A New Model of the Universe – Vantage Books

Priestley, J.B. (1964) Man & Time – Aldus Books Ltd.,

Prophet, Mark & Elizabeth (1988) The Lost Teachings of Jesus – Summit University

Rahula, Walpola (1959). What the Buddha Taught. NY: Grove Press

Ramana Maharshi (1972) The Collected Works – Rider, London

Ramana Maharshi (1984) Talks with Sri Ramana Maharshi – Sri Raman Sraman

Ray, Paul & Anderson, Sherry (2000) The Cultural Creatives – Three River Press, NY

Rinpoche, Sogyal (1993) The Tibetan Book of Living & Dying – Harper Collins

Ross, Hugh (1996) Beyond the Cosmos – Nav Press

Sadleir, Steven S. (1992) The Spiritual Seekers Guide – Allwan

Schuon, F. (1976) The Transcendent Unity of Religions – Harper and Row, NY.

Sekida, Katsuki (1975) Zen Training – Methods and Philosophy – Weatherhill

Sheldrake, R. (1981) A New Science of Life – Tarcher, LA.

Snelling, John (1991). The Buddhist Handbook. Rochester, VT: Inner Traditions..

Speeth, Kathleen R. (1976) The Gurdjieff Work – Pocket Books

Sumohadiwidjojo, Muhammad-Subuh (1975) Susila Budhi Dharma

Suzuki. D.T. (1970) Essays in Zen Buddhism – Rider, London

Tart, Charles, T. (1937) Open Mind, Discriminating Mind – Harper and Row

Teilhard, de Chardin P. (1961) The Phenomenon of Man – Harper, NY.

Temple R. Sirius Mystery

The Encyclopedia of Eastern Philosophy and Religion (1994). Boston: Shambhala.

Thomas, Lewis (1974) The Lives of a Cell – Bantam

Tillich, P (1967) A History of Christian Thought – Schuster

Tiwari, Maya (1995) Ayurveda – a life of balance – Healing Arts Press

Toynbee,A. (1972) A study of History – Oxford Univ.

Underhill, E. (1955) Mysticism – Meridian, NY

Walker, Kenneth (1942) Diagnosis of Man – Jonathan CAPE

Walker, Kenneth (1957) Patients and Doctors – Pelican

Walsch, Neale D. (1995) Conversations with God – Putnam

Watts, A. (1972) The Supreme Identity – Vintage, NY

Weber, M (1963) The sociology of Religion – Beacon, Boston.

Weinberg, Steven (1992) Dreams of a Final Theory – Pantheon Books

Wesselman, Hank (1995) Spirit Walker – Bantam

White, John (Ed) (1972) The Highest State of Consciousness – Anchor

White, John (Ed) (1974) What is Meditation – Anchor

Whitehead, A. (1967) Adventures of Ideas– MacMillan NY.

Wilber, Ken (999) One Taste – Shambala

Wilbur, Ken (1995) Sex, Ecology, Spirituality – Random

Wilson, Colin (1971) The Occult – a history – Random House

Wilson, Colin (1978) Mysteries – Hodder & Stoughton

Yogananda, Paramahamsa (1946) Autobiography of a Yogi

Yogananda, Paramahamsa (1946) Autobiography of a Yogi – Self realization

Zaehner, R. (1957) Mysticism, Sacred and Profane – Oxford Univ. NY.

Zukav, Gary (1979) The Dancing Wu Li Masters – Flamingo

FROM THE AUTHOR

I have completed the book and the happiness is doubled because it is Thanksgiving Day, November 25th 2004. I wish happiness to all those working on my book and of course to all the dear readers of my book!

I have mentioned in the book, of many obstacles I had to surmount in writing this book. Perhaps I received the revelations too early in my life that I had problems in communicating my spiritual experiences to others and decided to keep silent for the time being. I had to wait till I found the right words and the right conceptual background for communication.

When I joined the University. of Metaphysics and started reading for a Masters and Doctors degrees in Metaphysical Sciences, I came across a wealth of material confirming the validity of my experiences. The discovery of Richard Maurice Bucke's book "Cosmic Consciousness" cleared all my doubts. Here I found accurate descriptions parallel to my own spiritual experiences for the first time. These were collaborated by many other sources.

I now feel that there was purpose in the course of events and that this may be the right time for the book to be published. As I am not publishing this book with any money making motive, I have full faith that it will reach the right hands and fulfill its mission.

When my final surrender to my doubts was cleared by Ken Wilber's One Taste, I restarted with a firm determination. Then I discovered Xlibris, which enabled me to get this book out without delay.

July 2007:Let me try to share with readers a little of what I have learned since the publication of this book two years ago. For me one of the main sources of new knowledge was in the on line appendix to the magazine What Is Enlightenment in their website "WIEunbound", a gold mine of valuable information on spirituality.

I could agree with Eckhart Tolle that each human being is a cell of the Supreme Being and the need for each of us to integrate fully with one's being, which is identical with IT's Being. Our mental equipment is better left alone as it continues to distract us from the correct path. When Human Beings, Living Beings and Micro Beings (atoms and particles) interact with the Supreme Being IT takes their form temporarily to the delight of the lesser being.

In endeavouring to understand my relationship to whatever name is used to mean everything that exists e.g. Cosmos, I was happy to learn the Sanskrit sutra "Aham Brahmasmi" which means that I am identical with the Supreme Being.

To understand the nature of this relationship I selected the analogy of a giant sponge and its spores because if given a chance to grow freely each spore will in time be identical with the parent sponge which is equivalent to the Supreme Being.

Another subject that interested me was reincarnation. I was particularly interestesd in Ian Stevenson's research in Sri Lanka, see his book "Twenty Cases Suggestive of Reincarnation" published by the University of Virginia. My email addresses are lionelperera@comcast.net and sreeni_lionel3@verizon.net. Please keep in contact.

I have no space to mention the names of all those who helped me. I am grateful to all of them.

I have lived in over 50 countries, thanks to the United Nations and the Commonwealth Fund and

I cherish the friendships with my friends in all the countries I have lived in, including USA. Please keep in contact. I love you all.

Lionel Maithri Perera
3201 Unit 1, Grand Avenue
Everett, WA 98201
November 25, 2004